Becoming the

WORLD'S TOUGHEST LIFELONG LEARNER

About The Spaniard

Charlie "The Spaniard" Brenneman competed at the highest levels of mixed martial arts. **We can learn much from his experience in combat sports and life,** as he constantly strives to learn, grow and improve in every aspect. Get on the path.
Leif Babin
Former Navy SEAL Officer
New York Times **Bestselling Author**
See page 118

Charlie Brenneman believes that "Work Ethic = Dreams." Those are the exact words that are inscribed in my WWE Hall of Fame ring and something we both share. His new book is about working your a$$ off for what you want, while documenting the process. You want to achieve a Want, a Desire, a Dream, my brother Charlie can help you Live IT.
Diamond Dallas Page
WWE Hall of Famer
Creator, DDPY
See page 187

I meet a lot of people, and very few of them keep coming back. I met The Spaniard several years ago at our Spartan Wrestling Camp. He approached humbly and eager to learn. Since then, he has become part of our family. **It takes a unique person to live the Spartan code—continuously striving, pushing, enduring—and Charlie does it and loves it.** His love of learning and teaching shines through in his books, podcasts and speaking. He's not reached the success he aspires to just yet, but he will, and this book is documenting the process. Read it. Learn. And do!
Joe De Sena
Founder, Spartan
See page 49

Charlie's story is unique and his message is powerful. I knew his experience in and out of the octagon were unlike anyone I had seen before. But until we met in person, I didn't truly see how committed he was to being the World's Toughest Lifelong Learner. **With a blend of humility and boldness, he attacks every single day to get everything he can out if it.** There's simply no quit in this man ... an example for every one of us to follow.

Dave Berke
Retired Marine Corps Fighter Pilot
and TOPGUN Instructor
See page 116

I first heard Charlie on the *Spartan Up!* podcast, I was drawn in by his story and his character. His background was nothing out of the ordinary, just a good upbringing through family and wrestling, and a LOT of hard work. As a casual MMA fan, I recognized his nickname "The Spaniard." Little did I know that I would not only become an AVID listener of Charlie's own podcast but develop a friendship with him too. I started using his content with my students and athletes because **a message of joy, learning, and hard work couldn't come from a better source.** He's able to connect with young people because he's genuine: Charlie's done the hard work he's talking about. This is what separates "The Spaniard" from the crowd: His authenticity and his heart. When he's getting emotional during a story or geeking out over a book, it is 100% genuine. After reading this book, I can't guarantee you'll become friends with the Spaniard like I did, or become a UFC fighter like he did, but I can guarantee that you'll be fired up about learning! Charlie's the real deal. Let his work ethic and passion for learning and teaching inspire you!

Eric Pritchard
New Jersey high school teacher/coach
See page 167

Charlie's message has been a strong part of my daily life for the past five years or so. It's been sort of **a guiding light for me** at times. Charlie puts in the work and unselfishly shares his knowledge with as many people as he can. In this fight that we call life I like to think of him as my cornerman.

Adam Hluschak, *aka* **"Shakky Boy"**
Spaniard-coached wrestler turned
hospitality professional
See page 53

I've been following Charlie since his UFC debut, and he instantly became one of my biggest role models. I love his "fighter's mindset" and his incredibly positive outlook on life. As someone who suffers from anxiety and depression, **Charlie's consistent words of affirmation are just what I need to remind myself that everything will be OK and to never give up.** Although his content is aimed at the masses, I swear he always manages to say what I need to hear, exactly when I need to hear it. AMX has been part of my morning routine since Episode 1, and (for the first time in my life) I actually look forward to my alarm going off and opening up my Podcasts app to tune in!

Ashleigh Williamson
UFC fan turned friend
See page 203

When you provide a flower sunlight and water it grows and blossoms, but without that nourishment it wilts and dies. I view learning as the nourishment to our brain and soul. Learning is the core of all success. It gives us an edge to continuously improve. Without it we stop growing, life becomes dull, and others rise above and take our sunshine. That's why I start my day with The Spaniard. Charlie brings learning to life with a mix of personal experiences and knowledge passed down from experts and doers in a variety of topics. His nuggets of knowledge are relatable and thought provoking. **His passion for learning will bring you on a daily journey to be a better you.** I never know what I will get out of his teaching. It could be greater inspiration to push through a workout, how to be a better parent, friend or partner, or it could be how to incorporate the experiences of others to do better in your business. One day I was preparing for a big presentation, and listened to Charlie's podcast about Boom-Boom Mancini. The quote from his father about "creating a ripple" brought my presentation together. It became the home run in my sales pitch. Stick with the Spaniard! Keep listening and learning. You never know when and where you will learn something valuable to take you to a whole new level.

Marissa Hoover
Director of Development & Alumni Relations
Penn State Harrisburg
See page 32

Listening to Charlie's show every day and embracing his message of lifelong learning has enhanced my life in so many ways. Not only do I know more about the world and people around me, but I've been able to use that knowledge to live a happier, more productive life that reflects my goals and priorities. **Charlie's message is simple and one that he embodies: Learn and grow every day. The benefits of that message, though, are profound.** I couldn't be happier to also consider myself a proud lifelong learner, thanks to Charlie and his continued dedication and friendship.

Ben Coate
MMA journalist
See page 168

It takes a uniquely bold individual to announce his phone number on a podcast and invite anyone ready to stretch and reach their goals to call directly. In 2017, I listened to this man named "The Spaniard" announce his phone number, and he shared his willingness to connect with his listeners personally. Immediately, the Steve Jobs quote came to mind, "The people who are crazy enough to think that they can change the world are the ones who do." **I had to call this guy because I wanted to be surrounded by world changers.** And I DID call him! Charlie stays in front of me to ensure I'm the best version of myself. Whether he's in my ear sharing his insight on *The Spaniard Show* or sending a personal text encouraging me to "Be Bold," he is a trusted mentor and great friend. Charlie asks uncomfortable questions to help people get clear on what they want. He is "The World's Toughest Lifelong Learner," synthesizing all that he reads and learns to share knowledge with anyone willing to listen.

Chad Miller
Sales professional
See page 168

My team thoroughly enjoyed having The Spaniard attend our leadership conference. Charlie's authentic approach to sharing his message of life-long learning left us inspired and motivated to keep learning, keep moving, and to never quit!

Amanda Rondon
Northeast Regional Director
Team RWB

Charlie brings a vast amount of knowledge on a wide range of topics with content that is relatable and applicable to any listener. His upbeat attitude and unmatched positivity combine into incomparable passion that radiates to the listener. When asked for advice Charlie has greatly exceeded expectations by providing insight including additional supporting book quotes and references. Every listener is important to him and he puts forth any effort needed to encourage listeners to challenge themselves and optimize their lives. **His unique background and eagerness to learn combine and make him the most down-to-earth, interactive and effective host out there.** After absorbing his content it is impossible not to see increased positivity, discipline, desire to learn, excitement for life and courage to "just stinkin be you"!!

Torie Kirk
Triple-Trifecta Spartan Racer

He made me laugh.
He made me cry. He cried.
He helped me realize I am
stronger than I see myself.

Desiree Magee
Mitochondrial Disease Parent / Expert
Interviewed on *The Spaniard Show*
See page 206

Charlie has been **a huge influence in maintaining my determination to keep on working hard at my goals.** Through the evolution and growth of *The Spaniard Show* Charlie has turned up consistently and delivered inspirational, quality listening reviewing great books and inspiring me to read a few along the way. Listening to Charlie is the perfect way to ingest the very best parts of quality books without necessarily reading them myself.

Craig from Scotland
See page 168

Becoming the
WORLD'S TOUGHEST LIFELONG LEARNER

*A Book for Anyone
Who Wants to
Pursue Anything*

Charlie
"The Spaniard"
Brenneman

For Gracie and Rocky

INTRODUCTION

This book is a combination memoir and how-to. The
how-to part is about pursuing anything that matters to you.
The memoir part continues the story of My Unlikely Journey
from Classroom to Cage (subtitle of my first book, *DRIVEN*)
while sharing what I've learned in the past five years building the business that is The Spaniard. Much of the content of
this book comes from my podcast, *The Spaniard Show*. I wrote
it just in case, if you are new to me, you'd rather read a few
hundred pages here than start from Episode 1 and listen to
well over 800 hours of recording, as of the time of publica-
tion. You might consider this book a digest of *The Spaniard
Show*.

As you will see, my mission is to *embody* lifelong learning so as to *inspire* lifelong learning. Prior to, during, and / or
after reading this book, I encourage you to follow this saying
that I have come to use, to help fan the flame of learning:

Read a book
Take a pic
Tag me
@charliespaniard

Some quick notes about quotes: Throughout the book are
quotes from episodes of *The Spaniard Show*. The show is organized into different types of episodes, all of which start
with the letters "AMX" (explained on page 41). Many quotes

reference whatever book I discussed in that episode, but the quote might be my own words or the author's words or even a quote from another source. In each case, I did my best to clarify the source of the thought. Any quote that includes no reference comes from me. Think of each quote as a snippet of a transcript of that episode.

One final note about the Contents section: You will notice that some chapter numbers are not in order. That's on purpose, not a mistake. Because this book is meant to be a manual as much as a story, the contents are presented to help you find sections more easily when you use the book as a reference in your own pursuits.

Thanks for reading this. I hope you find learning that helps you.

— Spaniard

*For speaking and program info, as well as my reading list, please visit **charliespaniard.com***

Connect on social media

@charliespaniard

Listen on any podcast app

the Spaniard show

CONTENTS

PAGE **CHAPTER**

17   1   About The Title
22   2   Before The Title

Taking Action
29   3   How I figured out what to speak about
39   4   Why I'm documenting my career as I build it
59   6   Starting my podcast
120   12   How the podcast has developed
221   18   How I use my new and lasting system

What Guides Me
48   5   Vision
77   7   Purpose
88   8   Authenticity
98   9   Humility
103   10   Energy
109   11   Boldness
136   13   Perseverance
160   14   Belief
178   15   Connection
191   16   Preparation
210   17   Service

228   19   THE END of the Beginning

EXTRAS - Three Articles
235   Deep Dives: 3 Topics That Changed How I Think
241   Accountability Matters Even More Than I Thought
252   Figuring Out My Identity

255   Guests & Books Featured on *The Spaniard Show*

1

About The Title

I've been a questioner for as long as I can remember. (Sorry, family!) Asking questions is as much a part of me as my arms and legs. I just need to know, ya know? Though it's (ahem) annoyed many people over the years and has even caused some people to see me as condescending, this curiosity and need to know has served me well. It's enabled me to reach high levels in Division I wrestling, a world-class ranking in mixed martial arts, achieve near-native proficiency in the Spanish language, graduate college with a 3.985 QPA (not one B!), and write a book. (Well, two books now.) Though I can't quite say I've become a world-class speaker and podcaster just yet, I can tell you I'm using the exact same process I've always used to make it so.

I tell you all of this not to point out how special I am, rather the opposite. I tell you all of this to point out how unspecial I am, how all of my successes in life have been the direct result of my unwavering commitment to learning and asking questions and to never stopping. If you came looking for a secret, that's it. You can now close the book and carry on.

But if you're looking for more than that, if you're looking

to understand how an unspecial kid from small-town Holli-daysburg, Pennsylvania, became the WORLD'S TOUGHEST LIFELONG LEARNER, and how you can use all of those tools and experiences in your own way, to write your own story, to create your own thing—good! Too often we sit back and wait for *them* to do the thing, for *them* to win the title, for *them* to go to the place. *They* have what it takes, and we don't. Bollocks to that! As I'm proclaiming my WTLL title, I'm also issuing a friendly challenge, or rather, a call to a shared experience. Why should I, The Spaniard, hold the title World's Toughest Lifelong Learner? Why shouldn't you? Why is this never-ending quest for knowledge, and the spoils that go along with it, reserved for me, and not you? Answer: It's not. Grab that stinkin' seat belt and strap in. We're going for a ride!

The World's Toughest Lifelong Learner is an idea. It's the manifestation of everything I aspire to be: Mentally strong, physically tough, well-read, open and aware of ideas and perspectives that exist in the world and where I fit into them. It's the aim of being the smartest, coolest, toughest, nicest, most helpful, funniest person on Earth. It's a commitment to a never-ending quest to get the most out of life and yourself. To me, it's the point of being.

It's also you and me, real and tangible. It's what happens when you put in the work, reading books and asking questions, learning and evolving daily, figuring out who you are and what you stand for. It's going to the gym and working your body as you work your mind, believing fully that the two are connected. It's committing yourself to something bigger than yourself.

Being the World's Toughest Lifelong Learner means that you are putting good into the world. You are helping others as you help yourself. You radiate an energy that makes other people better. When you commit to becoming the World's Toughest Lifelong Learner, your being, simply *being*, the way you are, makes other people strive to be better.

Ironically, I spend a great deal of time having to explain exactly what I do for a living, even to my own family. My wife Amanda is entitled to know why book after book arrives on our doorstep and her husband spends his time reading them and taking notes. My parents would like to know what their former Spanish teacher / UFC fighter son does with his time. My siblings often joke about my not having a job. (Except it might not be a joke ... I'm still figuring out what my job is!)

An effect of having to often explain what I do for a living is that I often have to think about it and reassess: What *do* I do for a living? I have to put it into words that make sense to other people. And it's not easy to explain. In its simplest form, as Dread once put it to me, "I read books and talk about them."

"Wait," you might be asking yourself, "who's Dread?" If you're a fan of *The Spaniard Show*, you know that Dread is my sixth sense, my Mr. Miyagi, my shaman, my advisor, my friend, my partner, my sometimes co-host and a giant piece to the puzzle that I'm putting together. No joke (well, halfly no joke), I sometimes wonder if Dread really exists or if he's part of my consciousness—think *Fight Club*. I'd recommend scrolling all the way back to episode #1 of *The Spaniard Show*, and you'll hear us in our early glory, not even knowing we didn't know the things we would eventually know!

You'll hear more about Dread later. I brought him up because I was saying that he and I have often discussed what it is I do, and at one point his suggestion was simply, "You read books and talk about them."

That's where it started to develop. Books represent learning. They represent knowledge and wisdom. To my knowledge, inscribing on scrolls and tablets was an extension of the spoken word. It was a way for elders to pass on knowledge and history to future generations and to keep their piece of the pie, their time on Earth, going. From tablets and scrolls (and this is my informed guesstimation), books evolved. Note: When Dread read what I just wrote, he suggested I read a book on the history of books. I like it! That's how learning happens: You become aware of not knowing something you want to know, and you go get the knowledge.

To me, books are an adventure. They're fantasy and reality mixed into one. They are my escape into worlds and minds and stories to which I would have never been exposed. They are an opportunity for me to live hundreds of lives during my time here on Earth. Post-fighting, books became a controllable way for me to continue surrounding myself with world-class performers and thinkers, as I had done every day in the gym for nearly a decade.

In the past few years, I've gotten very comfortable saying that wrestling is who I am, and fighting is what I do . But as I progress in my new ventures, I find myself thinking that maybe learning is truly who I am.

So what then do I do? Out of all of this studying and thinking and talking emerged this idea of LIFELONG LEARNING.

Dread first brought it to the table. He would say that everyone knows lifelong learning is a vital part of life, as well as the focus of nearly all commencement speeches, and yet there is no one who personifies it. There is no poster child for lifelong learning. Meanwhile, I needed a "thing," something that I did or uniquely represented, something to build upon, and my "being" lifelong learning seemed as exciting as anything I could have imagined. It is the culmination of everything I do, and, ironically, it leads back to my roots in teaching Spanish. Back then, I guided students toward lifelong learning. Now I still do, just in a different way.

Dread and I started talking about how to give an interesting name to something that everyone knows but no one thinks about. Lifelong learning became a solid starting point from which to grow something that is universal and neverending, but I needed a way to talk about it. I needed something to make people say, "Hmmm, what's that about?"

I remember it as clear as day. Dread and I were talking on the phone, brainstorming, and at this time, I had already grown close with former WWE superstar and current youth speaker, Marc Mero. He had been mentoring me and sharing his wisdom on starting a speaking career and continues to do so to this day. Marc's handle in the speaking world is "America's #1 School Presenter," and if you follow him on social media (@marcmero), you'll see that it's true. Speaking with Dread on the phone and reflecting on everything Marc was teaching me, I thought, and said, "What if I was America's Toughest Lifelong Learner?" And Dread said, "America? Why not the world?"

And so the story begins ...

2

Before The Title

This book will tell you the whole story of how I became the World's Toughest Lifelong Learner, but first, let's go back. Not all the way back to the beginning, as I already wrote a book that does that.

I wrote my memoir *DRIVEN: My Unlikely Journey from Classroom to Cage* to answer the many questions I had gotten over the years after having left my Spanish teaching position to pursue professional fighting—and because I was about to be fired from the UFC and had nothing else productive to do. Getting the boot from the UFC was the impetus I needed to start looking forward, to consider where I would take my life next. I figured my story was a solid platform from which to launch a writing and speaking career (podcasting was not yet on my radar), so I ran (wrote) with it.

I'll give you a brief synopsis below in the event that one Spaniard book is your limit and you have no desire to pick up a copy of *DRIVEN* to read the entire story. Just be aware that that means I have no room to give you the juicy details about almost getting my eyeball kicked out of my head, picking a fight with the toughest man on the planet, being the hero and the zero within a span of months and having a stroke at age 29. My publisher won't allow it. Wait a minute, I am my publisher! What I mean is, I already wrote the book, but here are the highlights:

- Raised by great parents who instilled strong values

- Youngest of four siblings, all of whom are great people and taught me well

- Small-town PA kid whose life was wrestling

- Hard-working in the classroom as well

- Scared to death of getting in trouble

- Underachieved in wrestling because of self-doubt

- Was always good, but rarely great

- Finished D-I wrestling on a high note: Top 12 finish at nationals and 1st team All-Academic

- Got job teaching Spanish and coaching wrestling at my alma mater in Hollidaysburg, PA

- Quickly missed the competitive and disciplined lifestyle of wrestling

- Ran a marathon, was mediocre at it, and missed physically dominating and being dominated by people

- Got cast on, and won, a reality show: *Pros vs. Joes* on Spike TV

- Learned the correlation between work and confidence: The harder you work, the more confident you get (odd that it took me so long to really learn, eh?)

- Sky became the limit
- On a whim, decided to pursue the UFC when I saw a wrestler-friend of mine doing it
- Decided to use my wrestling nickname "Spaniard" as my fight name
- Signed to the UFC
- Ranked #7 in the world in 2011
- Won and lost and won and lost
- Quickly learned the real, brutal world of professional fighting
- Got fired from the UFC for the second time
- Thought, "Hmph, what now?"

At the end of *DRIVEN* I say the following: (I first drafted these words around December of 2014)

> *So here I am, sitting on my couch, ten days after my last fight, trying to figure out what's next in my life. I might be done fighting, my career with the UFC is most likely done forever, and I end this story just as I began it, asking myself, 'How can I make a life in which I am personally and financially free?' I'm not completely sure, but no matter how I am remembered as a fighter, I have personal satisfaction in knowing that I once sat in my classroom at the Hollidaysburg Area Junior High School and thought, 'Wouldn't it be cool to be a UFC fighter?'"*

Those were the last few sentences of my memoir, or at least my first memoir. Perhaps a more fitting description than "memoir" would be "the first of a series of chronological tellings of my life story." Perhaps even more fitting words would be "the first of a series of chronological tellings of my life story so that my children, Gracie and Rocky (and more kids, if they follow!) can learn how to love learning and get the most out of themselves."

With everything Dread and I produce, we envision Gracie and Rocky as my prime audience (you'll hear more about that later), but it is my hope that you, Reader, are an engaged audience as well.

As I mentioned, I wrote my first book because there were just so many questions that I'd been asked throughout the course of my career that I knew at least a few people would be interested in the story. Kind of like when I did a self-audit of my skills and found that wrestling lent itself to fighting, I did a self-audit of my life experiences and realized that they lent themselves to an entertaining and inspiring book. At the time of this writing, *DRIVEN* has 60 reviews and a 5-out-of-5-stars ratings on Amazon.

Before I was officially an author, I had another title: SPEAKER

Boy, using that word "speaker" felt odd to me at the beginning. Don't we all "speak"? Aren't we all "speakers"? Looking back, this was my first foray into learning as a professional. Up to that point, I had always just wrestled, and I naturally fell into Spanish. But speaking was something entirely new that I knew nothing about. Quickly, I learned that authors speak and speakers write. They go hand in hand: You write a book and then travel around talking about the book you wrote. Writing a book gives you some degree of credibility in that you've put your thoughts into a coherent-enough format to justify a book. Without arguing and defending the validity of that statement, it certainly has been used to establish a general rule. Without a doubt, the credibility of books and authors varies widely. What I love most about being the World's Toughest Lifelong Learner, continuously writing, speaking and recording, is that I'm forced to really crystallize what I think and feel because the words coming out of my mouth and / or making their way onto the paper / screen are out there for the world to hear and see. Tie in the idea of lifelong learning, and those things are bound to change as I continue to learn and grow. It's as scary as it is exciting.

So whether or not I would fight again, I did know that I would start to formulate some sort of formalized speaking message.

I also needed money to survive. I figured speaking was the way. Aside from occasional substitute teaching in the first month or two post-fighting, my "voice" was now my income, however I could transmute that into dollars.

How did I move into speaking?
Ready, Fire, Aim.

Maybe you've heard that phrase: "Ready-Fire-Aim." I learned it from a mentor of mine, Andy, and it has guided me since hearing it. Andy doesn't know for sure where he got it, but according to Forbes.com, the originators were Tom Peters and Rob Waterman in their book *In Search of Excellence*.

It's obviously a twist on the traditional "Ready, Aim, Fire," a chronological, intuitive, step-by-step process. "Ready,

Fire, Aim" plays on the idea of taking too much time aiming (planning) and suggests that we take action prior to being 100%-without-a-doubt-this-is-the-most-perfect-thing-in-the-world ready so we can get a read on where we're going. You can think of this as the antidote to "paralysis by analysis." I know for a fact that my re-teaching of this principle changed the way a listener-turned-friend of mine, Craig from Scotland, does life and business. Mind you, this is not to say you should aim for Mount Everest having never climbed so much as the hill in your backyard. I didn't walk out of my Spanish classroom in 2007 straight up to Anthony "Rumble" Johnson (he's a REALLY scary dude) and pick a fist fight. I trained and planned and readied myself and then went for it, step by step. Don't mistake Ready-Fire-Aim for doing something in which you are not competent. The point is, the sooner you can take action, even imperfectly, the sooner you will be on your way to competence.

I knew what I wanted to be—a speaker with a voice—so I sought out speaking opportunities. I called on my personal relationships, people who were in my circle, my network, and I asked if they knew of any speaking opportunities that would fit my story. Because I was formerly a teacher and coach, I knew many people in education. Early on, this was without a doubt the most effective way to secure paid speaking gigs.

From wrestling tournaments to every level of education, I began to get on stage and share my story. I learned very quickly that wrestling crowds, though "my people," were very tough. They made me work for it. To be honest, sometimes I felt like the wrestlers in the crowd looked at me like they looked at making weight ... not good. Either way, I did my best and forged ahead and cut my teeth on speaking.

Looking back on my first attempts, I was bad, very bad. But if I were to ever get good, I had to start. I got better. I do believe / buy into the idea that you've got to do your work (speak for free) before you can start reaping the benefits (getting paid to speak), but I truly believed that I "did the work" for the past lifetime and that my story could rival the best of them, and I wanted to get paid for it. And I was committed to getting dang good at telling it!

Depending on how you look at it, you could say I put the cart before the horse. I was making cold calls, sending emails and booking speaking events without fully knowing what I was doing. I am actually laughing right now as I type this, thinking of how uncomfortable and unnatural I sounded and came off in my early days of "business."

But there was no other way. I was depending on me to make a living. Nobody was calling, nobody was offering me money to do anything. I had to create it. From value props to elevator pitches to various renditions of my marketing materials, I'm sure I embarrassed myself a hundred times or more.

Oddly enough, I actually enjoy this type of uncomfortability (which technically isn't a word, but I use it often, so it's kind of a word). Uncomfortability, in general, is a perfect place for growth and improvement to occur. While it's certainly disconcerting when you suck at something as bad as I did / do at cold-calling and elevator-pitching, it's also a glowing reminder of how much better you can get, and that is a challenge. As a lifelong wrestler and fighter, I do love me a challenge.

Above all, to become a speaker and to have a voice in any capacity, I had to start speaking and sharing my story. Rather than wait and plan and wait and plan, I went straight at it. And quickly started to sharpen my aim.

3

How I Figured Out What To Speak About

Before I continue about speaking, let me tell you about tailing off from fighting.

I sat for almost two months between my last UFC fight and officially getting released (a nice way of saying "fired"). It took some time for decisions to come down from the top. In January 2015, I officially received my walking papers from the UFC and was left with the "What in the heck do I do now?" question that so many professional athletes face.

Up until the summer of 2015, I was still training, not certain if this new venture of speaking would be my livelihood or merely a secondary endeavor until my fighting career concluded. Initially, I made attempts at signing with another big organization, but for one reason or another, it didn't work out. I'd become more specific in my requests, as I was no longer a single twenty-something with no real responsibility nor anyone to whom I had to answer. I had a family and a future to think about.

More than anything, I was thinking about my brain—obsessing about it, really. Part of this was justified. I'd been stopped seven times in my professional career, once by a knockout and the others by TKO or submission. The other part was simply my obsessiveness. I was asking nearly everyone in my inner circle, "Did I take a lot of abuse in my career? Do you think I should retire?" Whether this was obsession or totally justified, it caused me to take a timeout and assess where I was going in my life.

Not having secured an offer from a major fight organization, I began to field offers from regional and local shows. Nothing panned out. Initially, I set my gauge at $10,000, meaning that I wouldn't fight for anything less than $5,000 to show and $5,000 more if I won. But the offers I was getting, even as an 11-fight UFC veteran, ranged from $1,000-$5,000. I have a realistic assessment of myself—I did lose my last three fights in the UFC—but if that was all I was worth, then the decision was made for me. I would instead dive headfirst into speaking and voicing my knowledge and experiences. The day trips to Philly and New Jersey for high-level training would stop. While a three-hour-plus daily commute used to be the be-all-and-end-all of my day, it now no longer made sense. I needed to make a living, and my gut was telling me to put fighting on the back burner.

Finding my system

No longer having that fight to look forward to and build up toward, I felt void. There was a big chunk missing. I felt like I did when I went from the intense, goal-DRIVEN, hard-working lifestyle of a Division I wrestler to the somewhat relaxed and laid back lifestyle of a junior / senior high school

Spanish teacher. I needed to manifest that feeling of an athletic contest into every day in order to feel complete. The way I did that was by breaking down the way I lived and developing a system that keeps me operating at an optimal level. I have incorporated discipline into various aspects of my life with daily practices and limitations to keep me feeling that sense of "earned by hard work." They range from early-morning wake up times, to nutrition (that includes cutting back on my weakness, Pepsi) to the way I train in the gym.

I had always heard that word "system" but never fully understood it. Now I know that it's an organized, consistent, intentional, conscious way of doing things. It doesn't have to be complex. My morning routine is a system. AMX (which you will hear much more about) is a system. The way I train is a system. The way I keep track of appointments on my calendar is a system. The way I learned Spanish and the way I teach Spanish to my kids, Gracie and Rocky—those are systems. The way I eat is a system. I remember reading in Ted Turner's book *Call Me Ted* that he wore Velcro shoes so as to not waste time tying laces. That was part of his efficiency system. Steve Jobs' simple wardrobe (black turtleneck, blue jeans) was the same kind of system.

When I started speaking, I learned that teaching your systems to others, assuming they are helpful and beneficial, was a thing. This was a foreign concept to me for much of my life, but when I really buckled down and asked myself how I could get the most out of my days and myself, systems and methods of organization started to shine through.

I knew I had value to share, but I needed to figure out a way to make it teachable. As I write this book, I'm in my umpteenth iteration, but Dread and I are figuring it out! In the end, some of me is systemized, and some of me is not.

I worked on capturing a teachable system, something I could stand up in front of an audience and talk about, learning points and takeaways I could align with my story to give the audience something to work with as they ventured back into their own lives.

Early on, my name for this was "Addicted to Excellence." Excellence is something that I've pursued my entire life. When I was young, I remember my parents instilling in my siblings and me, "Do the best you can in everything you do, and inspire others to do the same." They never came right out and said that, but it was an idea that I took from how we were raised. That mindset led me to strive for excellence on the wrestling mat and in the classroom, in the UFC and now as a man. It's a way of being.

The title "Addicted to Excellence" had an obvious issue, just not obvious to me at the time. It was brought to my attention by Marissa, a listener-turned-friend who works at our local Penn State branch campus. We were talking about setting up a student activities program, and she mentioned the negative connotation of the word "addicted." Made sense. I had never considered that and wasn't totally on board with switching it across all my platforms, but the here-and-now told me I should. We landed on "Culture of Excellence" and ran from there. I've since done a dozen or more workshops / speaking events at PSU Harrisburg that continue to evolve.

In time, I started to emphasize what I called The Five Elements of Excellence: Vision, Values, Success, Accountability and Surroundings. Even that final terminology came about after several iterations. I tell you this not to overwhelm you, but rather to show you how things work when you go after them Ready-Fire-Aim style.

My thinking has continued to evolve from this system in

a way that I will explain as we continue our journey (see Chapter 18). However, The Five Elements are still valuable. I identified them (or rather they organically revealed themselves) for a reason. The Five Elements are a foundation for anyone wanting to organize and structure their mind and life. They also make a great structure for mastermind groups, which are when two or more people come together and work toward a common goal, a practice first popularized in the book *Think and Grow Rich* by Napoleon Hill. Masterminds can revolve around becoming better parents or people, improving business, losing weight and getting healthy—any important goal. The idea is that everyone shares and brings to the table different ideas, best practices and experiences that can help the group improve in the predetermined focus area. I conducted masterminds around The Five Elements for stretches of five to six weeks with small groups. Throughout the week, I would send out emails with personal stories and anecdotes that revolved around that week's specific Element, and I would assign certain tasks / reflection points that forced action, and then we'd have a weekly mastermind conducted virtually / over the phone. One of my favorite pieces of feedback from this experience was, "It helps you stay in front of your own BS."

It's quite possible that I will release some kind of something (book, pamphlet, video, whatever) on The Five Elements in the future, but, for now, here are the basics:

The Five Elements

The Elements were derived from a lifetime of thinking and note-taking. At different periods of my life, I've taken notes and jotted down ideas, always with the aspiration of living a life worth sharing with others. At one point, from 9/26/06 until 8/22/11, I journaled every day to capture a snapshot of my life at the time. These notes and journals and my obsessive thinking and questions helped me arrive at—or recognize—a certain system of living. It's how I had lived my life. I didn't set out from birth with this system and live to make it work. Instead, I just lived, and the system showed itself through.

Upon arriving home from Brazil in 2014 after my most recent fight, I decided that I had a voice—a story to tell and "stuff to share." I took those notes and organized, shuffled, re-shuffled and re-organized them, and in the end I came up with the Five Elements of Excellence:

Vision
Where you want to go in your life. What drives you to get out of bed in the morning. That single thing that occupies your brain most.

Values
Your foundation. What you stand for. Your character.

Success
What it means to you. Fast car? Big house? Peace of mind?

Accountability
Ownership. Taking responsibility for your thoughts, words, actions, reality.

Surroundings
Surrounding yourself with the best.

This framework was a way to share my story with implementable tasks and philosophies.

The Five Elements of Excellence are not merely a package. By that, I mean that they're not something I created to sell a book or form a series of workshops. They are essentially the first rendition on paper of my actual being, of myself as a person. When I made the decision to enter speaking and teaching outside the classroom, I needed to figure out who I was and what I thought. That may sound silly, but when you are on a stage or behind a mic, you are forced to work your thoughts out into clearly transmittable and comprehendible words, phrases and ideas. If I was going to teach a system of living, I had to fully know that system. I needed to clearly identify and dissect the components (or Elements), and what I got were Vision, Values, Success, Accountability and Surroundings.

My system is my system. It's what works for me. It keeps me accountable. It pales in comparison to some of the approaches of people I know and read about, but I'm concerned with me here. I continue to upgrade and improve multiple areas of my life based on intuition and influences, and I will continue to seek a healthier, more efficient way of living as long as I'm alive.

I don't expect you to accept my particular approach with open arms, thoughtlessly adapting my thoughts and experiences as your own. I want you to attack it like I attacked my life, with a crap-ton of questions and an openness to learning. Let my thinking serve as the basis for your own thought and, ultimately, action.

Everything I do and share adds up to a life curriculum for living boldly. Selfishly, I am creating it as a guide for myself and, ultimately, my kids. It is my guide to fight the daily demons of negativity, self-doubt and fear that creep into my mind. It's my daily juice to face the day with A Fighter's Mindset (the original title of my podcast)—to get after it and confront it, armed with knowledge, wisdom and know-how to smash it. Because of this, little by little, *The Spaniard Show* is becoming more than a podcast, and World's Toughest Lifelong Learner is more than a title. It is becoming a way of life for myself and others.

I am creating the class I wish I would have had in school. I'm simultaneously learning and teaching what it takes to live BOLDLY (another earlier subtitle of my podcast was "Learn to Be Bold"). I am the teacher and the student. In my readings and conversations, I've learned that the best of the best don't have it all figured out. Or perhaps more accurately put, what they do have figured out is that they don't have it figured out. They are just like you and me.

> *I want to get whatever it is—whatever potential, whatever ability, whatever strength, whatever superpower it is—I want to get it out of you. That's my job. That's what fuels me every day.*
> **AMXbooks 142**

I moved forward with The Five Elements and trying to figure out how to get business and grow. I started talking and asking questions, and I continued reading, teaching, reflecting and repeating the process.

I looked for role models. Post-fighting, I found that I had grown accustomed to being around "world-classers" on a daily basis. I liked it, and I needed it. You don't become a world-classer by sitting on the sidelines, you become one by surrounding yourself with other world-classers. Since I no longer spent my days training alongside guys like Frankie Edgar, Eddie Alvarez and The Miller Brothers, I had to figure out another way to surround myself with like-minded people. I saw Tim Ferriss grow his podcast by systematically dissecting how things work, why they are what they are, and asking experts their best practices on a variety of topics. I saw Joe Rogan (with whom I align most) allow his natural curiosity to guide his podcast, The Joe Rogan Experience, to becoming one of the biggest there is. I saw him lead a dynamic life based on his strong skill set (host, comedian, commentator, athlete). I saw Jocko Willink rise to stardom and success in a domain new for him, since he was already a very successful Navy SEAL and officer. All of these people were stepping outside the conventional way of being. They built their own lives. I started that process when I left teaching to fight, and I was figuring out a way to continue riding that wave.

The three people I listed above have played prominent roles in helping me evolve. They are just three of the many. There are an infinite number of "experts" teaching this or that, but for me to really buy into someone, there needs to be a certain level of credibility. My personal preference is to learn from people who have been in the trenches physically, people who have put their bodies / lives / selves on the line— in the military, combat sports or sports in general. People who are survivors and adventurers. There's a level of credibility that comes from risk and overcoming adversity. I need to buy into what this person has overcome, done or learned. I suppose there's some simple taste or preference involved, too. Am I drawn to this person's story and energy? Gary Vaynerchuk likes to point out that some people teach business without ever having created a business. Those are the people I avoid—ones who put out lots of noise and production based on what, exactly? I fought in a cage for a living. I know the truth that arises from that experience. I know that my words are based on that truth, or at least an evolution of that truth, and I look for that in others.

I started to piece together this idea as I looked at others who had built something: If they can do it, I can do it. I knew that I had things to say. I knew they were valuable. I knew what I wanted. I could clearly see that it's possible to build a rewarding and meaningful career sharing what I've learned and continue to learn.

But how?

4

Why I'm Documenting My Career As I Build It

There are a lot of people that want to hang onto their secrets, but there's a lot of them that want to share them, just so you don't have to go through what they went through. That's why I'm really open about the early struggles.
Gorgeous George Garcia
MMA Host
AMXtalks 157

I'll tell you what I did as I moved forward. If you're a fan of *The Spaniard Show*, you're already listening to me telling you what I do as I move forward, present-tense. In case you aren't, I'll spell out the process: Every morning I wake up ... read / review my latest book (I just finished David Goggins' *Can't Hurt Me* and started Ross Edgley's *The World's Fittest Book*) ... lesson-plan for the show ... and then record, all while thinking things through out loud, updating on progress, teaching and interacting with my Facebook livestreamers. It's part of my system (AMX) that I mentioned earlier. What I'm doing here is thinking long-term: Do the work now—the ugly, dirty, smelly, hard, non-return-type stuff—so you can have what you want later. It's a version of Dave Ramsey's idea of living like no one else now so you can live like no one else later. My foundation as a human is set. I know what I value and who I am, but I allow my thinkings and learnings to continually shape and improve me. And yes, sometimes that results in shifting the way I think and feel about certain things. It's part of growing.

Say that I could go back to 2006-7, on the afternoon when I had that fateful conversation with my buddy Beardie after school ("One day, I'm going to fight in the UFC") and that I had recorded and written about everything up until my first fight in the UFC. That's what I'm doing this time. I'm chronicling the process of my next venture as I apply a tried-and-true methodology that consists of two four-letter words: HARD WORK. By keeping up to date with my thinking, reading and learning, I'm sharpening my presentation skills for when I'm on stage. Those who train will understand: My show is my reps. And for the small circle of true fans I have (and remember, for my kids), it's a way to share the evolution of my career in progress. Imagine if Tony Robbins had recorded his day-to-day learnings, progress and mindset as he developed into the world-wide success that he is today. How cool would it be to have that record?! *Ding ding ding ding ding*—that's what I'm creating.

A QUICK ASIDE: Explaining AMX

I'm referring to my "AMX system" enough that I need to explain. The earliest version of my show—on Facebook Live before I added it to the podcast—was me talking about books that I was reading. It was a daily show, and I simply called it "Daily Reading." Kind of a boring name, right? I ended up changing it to "AM Excellence," as in "Morning Excellence," and that was soon shortened to AMX. NOTE: When hashing out the terminology we would use (a weird thing in and of itself), I favored calling AM Excellence "AMEX," pronouncing it just like the credit card. Dread, thinking ahead, convinced me that AMX (pronounced by saying each letter: A M X) was the better option. It sounds like a system number (think P90X), and we find that it just works. In time, we extended it to the four tracks that make up The Spaniard Show. My show is four shows in one, as follows (episode times are approximate):

AMXbooks
I talk about lessons from books, 8 minutes, Monday - Friday

AMXkids
I talk about lessons from kids' books, 20 minutes, Tuesday

AMXtalks
Interviews with the aim of learning from the guest. This is also where I publish keynotes, solo talks (solosodes) or talks with Dread (Dreadisodes), 20 to 60 minutes, Thursday

AMXweekly
I re-teach 7 learning points from the week, 20 minutes, Saturday

It looks pretty coherent as written above, but as you read on you'll learn how arriving at that was anything but planned and efficient. It was a by-product of bumbling and doing.

For the purpose of the book, when I refer to an episode, I will act as if I was using the above format the entire time, but be aware that the neatness of today is built upon the messiness of yesterday.

This book will be a sort of real-time case study for building a business, and only time will tell the outcome.

The fact that I'm writing this story today, rather than at the culmination of my life and career is a bit odd. Why should you listen to me? I haven't created a multi-million dollar company. I am not famous—though I've tasted fame—and I battle with the same struggles as you do, every day of my life.

Well, what if that's the exact reason you should listen to me? I look at myself as a sort of conduit between the Rich & Famous and the Average Joe. As a result of hard work, perseverance and some luck, I've had the opportunity to experience a great deal in life at a relatively young age. I've sat next to and hung out with world champions and millionaires, even talked with a few billionaires, and picked the brains of some of the most successful, unique and interesting people in the world (see the Quick Aside below), and I want to put it out there for the world to consume. Most of all, I want to put it out there for my kids, and one day their kids, to call upon and reference in their own lives.

A QUICK ASIDE: Do you bring superstars home?
Speaking of hanging out with amazing people, I'm in a unique position in treading the line between the "rich and famous" and the normal / not-famous. Here's an

example: A few months ago as I write this, WWE Superstar Diamond Dallas Page (DDP) was doing a meet-and-greet with my hometown minor league baseball team, the Altoona Curve (August, 2018). I had interviewed and become friends with DDP and had arranged to meet up with him. Because my life goes in a thousand directions, and because it's complex and always changing, I tend to simplify things when talking with my parents. I just told my mom, "I'm coming home to see a buddy who's in town." My mom loves to cook, and I love to eat. She knows that home-cooked meals get me home (I'm easy to figure out), so she asked, "Are you and your friend planning on eating here? Should I make something?" It still warms my belly to think bringing DDP, WWE superstar, to my house to eat dinner with my parents! But by the same token, we've sat down and had meals with some of the most successful people on Earth (UFC champions, Olympians, really successful business people). It's a funny space in which to exist. (NOTE: My mom's biggest get, as well as mine, is The Rock. "Tell 'em I'll make 'em homemade spaghetti and meatballs!")

Starting a business after my fighting career saw me step into yet another arena in which I had no prior experience and might be hard to justify entering. The scene had changed from fighting, but the idea was the same: I had to fight tooth and nail (and I'm still scratching and clawing) for the respect and recognition that I believed was mine. The brutal truth is that no one cares—NO ONE—more about your success than you. I learned very quickly that I had to prove myself in this new arena. My fighting history might be enough to get me in the door, but I had to perform at an exceptional level to garner people's attention and earn the right to stay in the room.

I recently listened to actor Terry Crews on *The Tim Fer-*

riss Show podcast. He said something that I've been articulating in my mind for the past two years: "I want the vision of who I am and who I want to be to be out in real life. I want to back everything up with action. Back it up with movement." So what you're seeing is me putting the vision of who I am and who I want to be out in real life. I am backing it all up with action, causing transitions from one day to another-While linear progression is the last way that it might appear on a standard map, it is 100% the linear progression of The Spaniard. I am doing exactly what I'm supposed to be doing at this moment because I know no other way.

A QUICK ASIDE: Podcasting progress
Examples of episodes highlighting developments in the business:

This is one of those shows that shows the back-end part of it, the process, the journey, understanding that sometimes you win, sometimes you lose, but at the end of the day, you put your head down and keep moving forward.
A Key Change in The Fight Club
AMXtalks 64

Most of the frustrations that I deal with—the business challenges, the obstacles—are about metrics or numbers. The reason that my frustration is coming from them is that on those days, my mind is in the wrong place, my focus is on the wrong thing. If you take that outward, it's just reminding yourself: "Focus on what's important here. Focus on the process. Focus on the purpose. Focus on the value." That's where peace of mind comes from.
Podcasting with Purpose - Plus Possible New Titles
AMXtalks 89

Action begets action. Just start. You have your vision of your end goal? Just go.
Lessons from Podcasting: Year 1
AMXtalks 105

I mentioned that the show is my reps. I initially learned the importance of repetition and practice in wrestling. It all came down to doing the little things over and over again for years—decades—and having the appropriate people in place to remind me of what those important little things were. As my show is a guide for my kids, it matters a lot to me to demonstrate important practices in real time so that, if nothing else, they'll always have at least one place to look for guidance. It's like I'm teaching books and knowledge and experience, but also teaching the act of valuable habits such as commitment, consistency, authenticity, humility, energy, boldness, perseverance, belief and preparation. These are the things I want my kids to hear over and over when I'm long gone. And from whom, most of all, do I want them to hear them?! Me, their father! Think of it as when-I'm-gone-parenting. Can you imagine having a way to hear your parents tell you that *one thing* one more time, or a way to hear what your grandparents thought of this or that? Or simply to have the comfort of hearing their voices. I used to watch old home videos of my parents and family way back when. These episodes will be a daily version of that.

I have to live it

This blending of taking action and teaching also means taking on a responsibility to live what I teach, to be in alignment, to walk the walk.

When you start talking so much in a public forum—on

stage, behind the mic, on videos, so many places—you begin to realize the importance of living the code you are teaching. I began to hold myself accountable to anyone who would follow me. I was saying, "Follow me as I figure this out. I'll lead you someplace good." That's bold, for certain, and I'm sure that some people will say it's egotistical. I once had someone tell me, "That's the most egotistical thing I've ever heard" when I mentioned naming my show after some variation of The Spaniard. So be it. I simply know my mission: (1) Provide a blueprint for my kids to live their best life, (2) Satiate my thirst for learning and curiosity, and (3) Document it all so others can benefit.

Accountability has always been an important part of my life. When we were young, my parents taught us the importance of honesty and loyalty and respect—that you were accountable for your actions. My dad ruled with enough discipline to let us know we weren't to cross the line. He rarely had to raise a hand because we had been taught so well. That's not to say we never got in trouble. We just knew where the line was in the sand, and we rarely crossed it. The consequences were made very clear.

I'm extremely grateful that anyone would care what I say or do or think. It's humbling. I'm blessed to have had the experiences I've had, and to get to share them, and my love of learning and teaching has enabled me to take that even further. The value doesn't stop with me and my experiences. It continues, and it will continue to continue, in books, podcasts, interviews, documentaries and whatever other sources of inspiration that we create. But it won't work unless I do. Momentum will not carry this lifelong learning ship through, only daily work will. When I look back at the true followers, the 1 or 2% that I've gained in the past few years, I hold them in a place that is unique unto themselves. They're not family, and they're not friends (though several have become listener-turned-friends, but even that's different). Mostly, they're strangers who've put their faith in me to lead them to some place, and I hold that responsibility high. I am accountable to them to provide a path, a way, a guide. I'm accountable to show up, to do what I teach. Day in and day out. And if you remember, who's at the centerpiece of everything I create? Gracie and Rocky. What that means is that I'll only give you my best, because it's my kids we're talking about.

Here's how I think about my responsibility to listeners: I'm a dude who loves to learn and teach. I'm nervous and scared and doubtful, but I do the things that make me nervous and scared and doubtful anyway. I'm going to get online / on screen / on stage every day and do what I do because I learned from fighting that by doing what I do, I can inspire and connect with people. Marketers talk about testing, and that's my testing. I did this thing (pursued fighting) and saw this result (I connected with and inspired people). That, to me, is awesome. It's a blessing God has given me. And I know it's a full-time job for me to work through my fears and apprehensions, and if it's full-time for me (and essentially everyone I've ever met), it's likely full-time for you, too. So I've chosen to put a stake in the ground and say, "I'll be here every day learning and fighting through my insecurities in my 'lifelong pursuit of the ideal' (quoting George Pocock in the book *The Boys in the Boat*)." If you'd like to join me, come on in! Door's always open! Welcome to the family!

5

What Guides Me

VISION

I'm about to talk about vision, one of the original Five Elements of Excellence. It's not only still valid to me, but vital.

Thinking big is not reserved for *them*. It's for me and you. And to think big, to really think big, you have to know where you're going. "Hope is not a strategy" is something I've been reminded of more than once on this journey. Hope is too vague. You have to be precise about what you want. Success takes work, but let's even take that a step further—it takes organized and structured work. You need to have an understanding of what you're doing, and why you're doing it. (See the book *Start with Why* by Simon Sinek.)

Just today, on AMXbooks 632, I spoke of Joe Rantz, gold medalist in rowing at the 1936 Berlin Olympics (and the primary figure in the book *The Boys in the Boat*) and his coaches' need to fully understand why Joe did what he did. He had the greatest of gifts and abilities but not the consistency to fully realize his potential. His coaches began to dig into what made Joe tick. The lessons from Joe's journey are some of the most valuable you'll ever find. Your vision is where you're going and who you aspire to be. It's at the core of everything you do. It's your guiding light. In time, Joe was able to identify what lay at his core.

Another Joe—Joe De Sena (AMXtalks 70), founder of Spartan and author of *The Spartan Way*, which I covered on AMXbooks 571 through 577—calls this your True North. Without a vision, you'll have no direction.

As I moved forward with speaking and podcasting, my vision started to organically formulate itself more clearly. It evolved as I evolved. When I first started, my vision was simply to share my story and message. The format was essentially to use my personal experience and the lessons I had learned to help other people fight through their own challenges and overcome their own fears. There's a comforting togetherness and camaraderie that exists with sharing, and my vision was to share and provide that comfort and camaraderie.

I'll continue to explain the vision that I had as I moved forward with speaking and podcasting, but first, here's a powerful story from my show. It starts with a vision, and it ends with a result that surprised even the person with the vision: Joe De Sena.

I remember going up to Joe's Spartan Wrestling Camp in Vermont as an instructor and being in a group climbing a mountainside that basically had a staircase of rocks. These rocks were big and were not just naturally there. Someone had to have put them in place. My curiosity was piqued: "How in the heck did they get here?" The trail is one mile long, and without a doubt, it took A LOT of work to make these steps. I asked Joe about its history. He explained that it went back to how he loved training in stairwells in city buildings. When he ended up living on a farm in Vermont, there were no tall buildings, and he missed the stairwells. He got the crazy idea of a project like the Egyptian pyramids: Getting several thousand large stones and having race participants drag them up the nearby mountain. Spartan is all about taking on challenges that might seem impossible, and Joe honestly didn't know whether this was possible. He had a background in masonry, and his fallback plan was to place the stones using heavy equipment. He provided 300 race participants with pipes, ropes and straps and set them this goal before the start of the race: Build the stairwell. It all happened in one long day.

"I would have bet you a million dollars that there was no way they could do this," Joe told me on my podcast, "but they put a stone staircase in place, one mile long, from the bottom of the mountain to the top. Some of those stones are the size of small Volkswagens. It was unbelievable."

The power of a vision is something special. When I visualize how I want to spend the rest of my life, all the hopes and dreams and awesome adventures I want to have, I don't just do it as a way to escape reality. I visualize to know exactly where I am going. If you don't know where you're going, how are you going to get there?

Think about it this way: As is often said, you'd rarely take a long trip without a map or GPS, and it's much more efficient to head to the grocery store with a list. Just like a vision, GPS and a grocery list lead you to where you want to go, whether we're talking highways, aisles, or, in the bigger picture, life. When I was fifteen, my road map of life looked much different than it does now. If my mom would have sent me to the grocery store as a kid, our family would've been eating nothing but Cinnamon Toast Crunch and triple-decker PB&J's and drinking nothing but sugar.

Let's take it to the other extreme. In one of the most powerful books I've ever read, *Man's Search for Meaning*, Viktor Frankl, Holocaust survivor, psychiatrist and author said, "Mental health is based on a certain degree of tension, the tension between what one has already achieved and what one still ought to accomplish, or the gap between what one is and what one should become." The gap between what you are and what you want to become is the foundation of creating your vision.

Creating a vision is an intentional process. We often have big plans and dreams, but life gets in the way. I have a different suggestion: Allow your big plans and dreams to get in the way of life.

Creating your vision is essentially the starting point of writing your own story. Remember the *Choose Your Own Adventure* books from when you were a kid? You had the ability to write the story as you chose your own adventure. The recipe was simple: You made a choice, and your adventure was written. The story wrote itself as you chose one thing over another. Think of your life in a similar way. All of the choices you are making on a minute-by-minute basis are culminating in the adventure (or non-adventure) that you live.

A hero is a vision

One way to have / form a vision is by having a role model—or several. I still, to this day at 38 years old, prefer to call them heroes. I'm aware enough to know that heroes are mortals and make mistakes, but that word conjures up nostalgia and energy that keeps me crankin'! Regardless of how you want to identify them, find someone to follow.

Growing up, I was always taught to be myself, to be an individual and to not just follow the crowd. I agree whole-heartedly with that advice and will pass it on to my children, but, at the same time, I'll also encourage them to consistently look for people to strive to be like ... and be like them!

I was about six years old the first time I saw Rocky (my all-time hero) running through the streets of Philadelphia on screen, and, without knowing it, I was creating my vision. Everything about him—his story, the people in his life, the adversaries that stood in front of him, the wins and losses—all just clicked and made sense to me. Once after karaoking Enrique Iglesias on an AMXbooks episode, I quoted good ol' Rocky Balboa when my wife asked why I had to be such a dork: "I'm a dork, Amanda. That's what you married. We can't change what we are." I think Rocky might have said "fighter" instead of "dork," but you get the drift.

In my relatively short time on Earth I've learned that creating, but more importantly, living, your vision is at the forefront of a meaningful existence. Your vision truly is your driver, and it can change as you change. I've had a lifelong vision of being Rocky Balboa, and that vision has transmuted itself in various ways: wrestler, fighter, speaker, creator, World's Toughest Lifelong Learner. I have a fire that's burning deep within, and there's nothing that will stop it. One way or another, it will shine through. (It might also shine through that paragraph that I was thinking of Survivor's "Burning Heart" from Rocky IV.)

Since becoming a professional learner, I've had the opportunity to learn from and formulate new heroes and role models. Present day, here and now as I sit writing in my local Panera, Mister Rogers and Milton Hershey are shaping my vision as much as anyone. Combining the acts of bringing people lifelong education, like Mister Rogers did, and happiness, like Milton Hershey did, is enough to get me out of bed long before dawn on even the coldest and darkest winter mornings.

As I entered speaking, writing and podcasting, my initial vision of sharing my story to help others overcome their fears and challenges took on a new component: A vision to become a type of walking library. I had read in *The Talent Code* the idea of a coach being a matrix of experience and insight. I thought that was awesome. It created in my mind this image of a giant web of interconnected books, references, facts, quotes, people and advice that someone (you and I) could program into our brains and be able to recall, spontaneously and automatically, when called upon.

So yes, my vision is to become a walking, talking matrix of information so that I can help you operate better and more efficiently as a human being in a wide variety of areas. I have concluded many of my episodes by saying, "I want you to want to read a book" and that falls in line with becoming a matrix of information.

Here's an example of how I recommended the experience to a friend, Adam Hluschak (Shak, Shakky Boy), a former wrestler whom I coached in college. He is a high-achieving, goal-oriented individual who was looking for something more out of life post-wrestling. Comfortably employed, he was looking for a way to operate at a higher-level personally and professionally. Shak (AMXtalks 116) enjoyed college for all of the reasons most people enjoy college—he is / was a fun guy to be around. He's the life of the party. When we started working together, we outlined a set of daily / weekly anchors (a concept I borrowed from The Rock) that would help keep him on track. When you're wrestling / fighting / pursuing any set objective, there are dates, deadlines and other targets that keep you moving toward your goal. In the real world, that often gets lost in the noise that is every day. The anchors that Shak and I established for him included training, nutrition, listening to / summarizing my daily episodes and reading.

Anyone who knows Shak would know how crazy that sounds. Reading was the last thing he would ever do. I emphasized the importance of it and provided a selection of books that I knew would resonate with his being. I told him, "All of these things you read, you'll just start referencing them and using examples that you didn't even know you knew. They will become you."

And so they have. Shak uses his new wisdom to lead more effectively in his profession, and we regularly talk books in texts and conversations. He has totally bought into my system and the power of Surrounding Yourself with the Best (one of the Five Elements, remember) and has been influencing those around him as a result.

Why become a walking library and a matrix of information? The whole idea developed organically. Reading became a way for me to quiet and stimulate my brain at the same time. Post-fighting, I had all this extra time and energy, and I'm not referring to physical energy. It was more like an energy of being: 99.9% of myself used to be put into one thing—fighting—but now, there was essentially nothing. As I weaned off of fight training, I slowly began to find my way in what we'd generally refer to as a "normal" gym. I slowly developed an evolving system of training that replicated the physical and psychological benefits of fight training. It's comprised of bodyweight exercises, reps per minute, some traditional weights, running (long distance and interval) sprints, kettlebells, a Bulgarian bag, trail running and, by the time of this book's printing, I'm sure a few more things. And it followed suit: I needed to replace my physical energy with a worthy task. Maybe I was searching for a restructuring of self to achieve wholeness.

The point of becoming this walking, talking matrix of information was not to become a know-it-all. At the beginning, I didn't even know there was a point. I was simply keeping busy because I had nothing else to do, and I had segued into a speaking career that didn't entail too much speaking. Eventually, the idea of teaching began to surface, along with the intrinsic joy I get from the actual act of teaching. This resulted in a perfectly-aligned relationship: Learn as much as I can, and then teach it on stage and via my show.

Whenever I go back to my favorite Milton Hershey quote—"One is only happy in proportion as he makes others feel happy"—I start to connect things:

- My young self's yearning to help stores with "Help Wanted" signs (I would see the signs and feel bad, thinking that they needed customers to stay open)

- My internal desire to help and stick up for those who can't stick up for themselves

- The values my parents instilled in me

- My superpowers of discipline and ability to work

- The smiles and appreciation I saw in others when I spoke and taught

- How I was slowly developing a unique type of entertainment (I came to think of it as: An actor acts,

a musician plays music, a comedian tells jokes, I tell
learning)

• My innate curiosity and appreciation for learning

What was revealing itself was the early manifestation of
the World's Toughest Lifelong Learner. I simply enjoy making
people happy, and learning and teaching was (is) my way of
doing it.

The idea of WTLL, and lifelong learning in general, is
about a pursuit of the ideal. I remember first recognizing that
idea when reading Aubrey Marcus' book *Own the Day, Own
Your Life*. He is the founder of Onnit, a company that provides "foundations to support your human journey." I really
started to internalize Onnit's slogan, "Total Human Optimiza-
tion." Optimizing myself, in every area, is at the base of my
being and my learning: What can I learn from this person or
that story that I can apply to my own life to move the needle
forward? How can I get closer and closer to my ideal? My ideal being that when I close my eyes for the last time on this
Earth, I can do so with the "peace of mind which is a direct
result of self-satisfaction in knowing I did my best to become
the best I am capable of becoming." (quoting John Wooden's
definition of success)

Being the WTLL is about understanding the world
around you and your place in it. It's about understanding
YOU. I can say with 100% confidence that pursuing learning
has improved me as a father, husband, speaker, teacher, son,
sibling and listener. I've become healthier physically, mentally and emotionally. I've gained an awareness of history
(American and world), nature, food sources and ingredients,
kids' books and the gold that lies within them, and a whole
slew of other areas. I've become an overall better human and

communicator. I'm asking that you simply consider: "Hmmm, if this guy improved in all these areas simply by reading and asking questions, maybe I could, too ..."

Just don't stop

In the past few years, Dread and I must have had a hundred different "THIS IS IT! WE DID IT! GOLD!" moments that "up and vanished like a fart in the wind" (*Shawshank Redemption*). As we continued to bumble our way forward, I began to realize that the most common reason people don't accomplish what they aim for is simply because they stop. They give up. While there are certainly other causes of failure, I've seen this as often as any. And after reading hundreds of books and intensely studying success, stopping seems to be the most common enemy of success. One of the most memorable lines I've ever read was in *Shoe Dog* by Phil Knight, founder of Nike: "Just keep going. Don't stop." He said it was the best advice he ever gave himself and has to give. Committing yourself to lifelong learning is about making progress toward your goals. It's about setting your target on a worthy pursuit. I firmly believe that learning gets you what you want. Never stop learning. Never give up what you want.

The bonus of all of this is that I simply love to learn. I love the diligence of it. In reference to Muay Thai, my former trainer Justin said I was the most diligent student he's ever had. I enjoy the process of sitting down, slowing down, reading a book, taking notes, transmuting and connecting those notes outward to the audience and also to other learnings, making a lesson plan and sharing it. That, to me, is absolute freedom. It helps me, and it helps everyone who listens. That's what you call a win-win.

The other side of this, and part of the reason I wrote this book, is because I very much enjoy excellence. I enjoy experiences. I enjoy travels—beaches, mountains, other countries and cultures. I enjoy good food. I love beach houses. I envision a studio / gym that is essentially my grown-up playground. I aspire to expose my kids to all that life has to offer. But reality is such that what I envision requires dinero, a lot of dinero, so I've got to find a way to make lots of dinero. Because I believe learning will get me what I want, I've got to learn how to make all of that happen.

Another part of my vision, and business model, was / is to have a successful podcast. I learned the ease of producing podcasts with today's technology and distribution systems, and I quickly saw that I had a megaphone that could reach the entire world, even if the world had no idea! I was out there. To me, it just made sense that a podcast was a vital part of my future, so I set out to create one.

Starting my podcast

Ben and Jerry did not have a grand plan beyond "We're going to open a homemade ice cream parlor, and we're going to make ice cream in a rock salt and ice freezer." One thing leads to another.
Fred "Chico" Lager
Former CEO, Ben & Jerry's
AMXtalks 174

Success Principle #13: Take Action
Jack Canfield
The Success Principles
AMXbooks 426

So here I was starting a business without knowing anything about starting a business. It still feels odd to say, "my business," because, truthfully, I'm just building me as a human ... and trying my darnedest to make money in that process. I wanted and needed it to be sustainable. I've learned enough truths in my life to know I am not cut out to work in a traditional setting doing traditional things. Toward the end of my teaching career, I felt like a lion in a cage. Truthfully, today, I still feel like a lion in a cage a good bit of the time. I'm at a point in my business that is further along than last year at this time, but I'm still in the dirt (as per Gary Vaynerchuk's "Clouds and Dirt").

Podcasting seemed like a good thing to start doing. I was familiar with podcasts from listening to them. I remember when I first learned that they were free. FREE! I couldn't believe it. My buddy, Matt (whom you may know from *DRIVEN*), told me how to download them from iTunes, and I was like, "Umm, okay, but how much do they cost?" I absolutely couldn't believe that they're free. PODCASTS ARE ONE OF THE BEST LEARNING TOOLS OUT THERE.

When I talk podcasting with the general public, I'd say a good 60% don't know what I'm talking about. It's a curious mix of location, lifestyle, age and tech know-how that exposes people to the gold that is podcasts. In Central PA and nearby, I've found that the 40ish and older folks, and the college and younger folks, aren't all too familiar with podcasts. On-demand radio is a great way to explain what a podcast is. I still make sure I upload everything to my site for the people who aren't tech-savvy. I'm trying to make my podcast as easy as possible to consume for my parents, and people like them.

I almost immediately began to appear on other people's podcasts because I remember hearing how key it was to building awareness of who you are and what you do. During 2015 and through 2017, I appeared on approximately 70 podcasts, which was great, except that I was real-time figuring out what I was doing post-fighting. I hadn't even come close to grasping that I am indeed selling something, so I sure as heck didn't know what it was. When I entered this world after fighting, I was first exposed to speakers, performance coaches, courses, masterminds and information products, so I naturally started there. It was all so foreign and new, but I just went with it. I took action.

I had learned a simple truth from fighting: Get famous, and money and opportunities will come your way. Get kinda-famous, and kinda-money and opportunities will come your way. Be not-famous, and no money and no opportunities will come your way. At that point, you gotta work very strategically to make people take notice of you. It's all reversed: They don't come to you, you have to go to them. It's much easier when they come to you, so stop reading and go get famous! Joking ... kinda.

I wanted to build a personal brand around The Spaniard. The word "brand" is subject to a good bit of dispute and discussion. Some people whose livelihood is essentially being themselves disdain the word. Others proclaim it. Still others, myself included, use it when it's the most accurate word for what I'm describing. As per emotivebrand.com, some relevant definitions of brand are: "the intangible sum of a product's attributes" (David Ogilvy), "a person's perception of a product, service, experience, or organization," and "a person's gut feeling about a product, service, or organization" (both quotes from a *Dictionary of Brand* by Marty Neumeier). In no way do I think of myself as anything other than a guy who likes to be himself and aims to make a living off of it, so my usage of the word "brand" is simply due to ease of communication and convenience. And a podcast seemed a good way to build a brand.

Slowly, the idea of starting my own podcast became

more and more prominent. But, heck, I was nervous. This stuff is the real deal. It sounded high-tech. I started with no knowledge of how to create one. I could only imagine the technical know-how that must go along with creating one, and the thousands of dollars I'd have to spend and the expertise I'd have to acquire to follow through with it. None of which is true.

I vividly remember my first conversations with my fellow podcasting buddy, Jim Harshaw, about Call Recorder for Skype, how it automatically pops up when you make a call, how you simply click "record" and continue talking, how the audio file appears upon completing the call, how you simply export the file to your desktop, how you then upload it to your podcast host and then how iTunes sweeps it from there. That right there, my friends, is how you start a podcast, and it's essentially the same system that I used to produce 1000 episodes in my first 898 days. There is the process of setting up an account on a podcast host and of submitting and being approved on iTunes, but you can learn that through a simple Google search. You should also buy a microphone, but don't worry, the ATR2100 mic was recommended by some of the best in the biz, and it costs $67.95 on Amazon as of the moment I'm writing. Dread and I learned how to start a podcast just like we learned to self-publish a book: We just did it.

It's okay to not know much about what you are doing. It's basically the essence of life. We've all heard the reference to babies learning to walk, how their inner discovery and lack of inhibitions nudges them forward. Remember, the baby version of you had no fear. If you just keep that infant mindset, you can learn anything. There's a dichotomy that exists in learning, though, and you don't want to get caught in the middle. Don't get stagnant by gathering knowledge and not doing anything with it. It's oh-so-comfortable to sit and gather information while knowing full well you should actually be doing something with that information.

Even as you learn the absolute basics and prepare to start, you have to know that you actually WILL start. Stephen King said as much in his book *On Writing*:

> *If you can take it seriously, we can do business. If you can't or won't, it's time for you to close the book and do something else.*
> **Stephen King**
> **On Writing**
> *AMXbooks 529*

And King makes a point of telling us about his stacks of rejections from publishers and his own small beginning:

> *By the time I was 14 … the nail in my wall would no longer support the weight of the rejection slips impaled upon it. I replaced the nail with a spike and went on writing.*
> **Stephen King**
> **On Writing**
> *AMXbooks 523*

> *Four stories. A quarter apiece. That was the first buck I made in the business.*
> **Stephen King**
> **On Writing**
> *AMXbooks 522*

I didn't let fear hold me back

If there were a Kingdom of Fears, and the Kingdom of Fears had a king, his name would be King Spaniard. I've been afraid for as long as I can remember. The irrational "they think I'm going to steal something from the store, so look like you're not going to steal something" type of fear. When you start something new, a lot can prey on your mind: "I'll make mistakes and look dumb. I'll embarrass myself. I could fall short of my goals and damage my ego / reputation. I'll totally waste my time. Is this even a good idea? Am I better off now than I could be? Should I just stay still? I'm dizzy. This is terrible. Ugh, I wish I were content!"

> *I really and truly am afraid of nearly everything. I'm afraid of fighting. I'm afraid of getting in trouble. I'm afraid of saying something that's going to offend someone. I think I operate on fear. But the important thing to recognize is: It doesn't stop me from doing anything.*
> **AMXtalks 164**

There will always be fear, even when you're doing something that you've done before. It's much in line with the fact as any wrestler or fighter will tell you, that regardless of how many times you cut weight, it will never not suck. It will never be enjoyable. You'll just learn to deal with it better. Fear operates in much the same way. For me, and anyone else I've ever spoken to, been around, or heard speak about fear, it never goes away. Rather, your training and preparation displace the fear and move it into the corner with Baby (*Dirty Dancing*). One of my former coaches who also happens to be one of the best wrestlers in American history, Cary Kolat (AMXtalks 58), described removing doubt and negative thoughts as filtering and compartmentalizing. If you knew Cary, you'd rest assured, because if someone as tough and hard as him has doubts, you're just fine.

For me, the fear I felt in wrestling was much different than the fear I felt in fighting. Honestly, there was much less fear in fighting. I don't even know if I'd call it fear. It was more of a logical apprehension or assessment of the risks I was undertaking. In wrestling, my whole life depended on it. My hopes and dreams rested on winning. Fighting was much more pragmatic. There were ways to get around a loss, and as high school and college wrestling inevitably ends, fighting could hypothetically go on forever. It was never really over until I decided it was over. Wrestling was over when my eligibility was up.

My words above about fighters feeling fear aren't just wordplay and self-comfort. The enigmatic, hilarious, notorious Chael "The American Gangster" Sonnen was a guest on my show (AMXtalks 148). He's one of the best personalities to have ever fought in mixed martial arts. He also happens to be a former Division I wrestler and All-American and one of my wife's favorite fighters (there were a handful who I think she liked better than me, including Frankie Edgar [AMXtalks 24], Patrick Cote and Jon Fitch [AMXtalks 232] as well). He couldn't have said it any better regarding what goes on inside our heads at go-time:

> One thing that people don't know—because as fighters we don't let them in on it—but we're scared to death. It's one of the worst experiences. You're looking calm, you're looking cool, you've got your shirt off, you're on TV, and inside you're just, "Oh my God, can we just get this over with?"

I talked on one episode about my legs aching prior to running the 2018 Spartan World Championships in Lake Tahoe (30 obstacles / 13.5 miles ... I was not competing for the

championship. I ran in the open division.) These were the
same leg aches that used to hit me during my career. Something would change physiologically in my body that would
let me know: This is real, it's about to go down. The aches
normally started on Tuesday of fight week, the day we ar-
rived at the fighter hotel. It took me a while to figure out that
it wasn't that I was tired and / or overworked. My body was
just telling me something—getting into serious mode. In fighting, I learned to listen to my training, not my legs. That lesson
helped me run a successful Spartan race. Throbbing legs are
my own version of what Dean Karnazes described in *The
Road to Sparta*:

> *Karnazes describes his first marathon as "a raw con-
> frontation of self."*
> **Dean Karnazes**
> **The Road to Sparta**
> *AMXbooks 280*

I've listened to several interviews with Jamie Foxx, and
on one of them, I heard him say that "on the other side of fear
is nothing." That is to say, once you just lean into it (Success
Principle #14 / Jack Canfield), you'll find your fears aren't all
that bad after all. It's the apprehension and trepidation be-
forehand that, many times, is the worst part. Another great
book to note regarding fear is Jocko Willink's kids' book
Mikey and the Dragons. Mikey learns about looking fear in
the eye and the reality of many of our fears, which is often
times less than we imagine.

If we flip the script, we can also see that on the other
side of fear is ... everything. Everything you ever wanted is
beyond your fears. If fighting gave me one thing, it was freedom. I leaned into my biggest fear (fighting) with every ounce

of drive and ambition that I possessed and welcomed it with two fists. You can do the same. You just have to start.

I didn't let criticism hold me back

(Quote from Elbert Hubbard) To avoid criticism, do nothing, say nothing, be nothing.
Steven Pressfield
The War of Art
AMXbooks 370

When I speak on stage, I often share screenshots and quotes that I received via social media during my fighting career. They are the quintessential example of a life without accountability. What kind of person would go out of their way to attack a professional fighter, someone who fights people for a living? The kind that will never have to answer the bell, that's who. Here are a few of my favorites:

> *@CharlieBrennabad I once saw a spaniard get knocked the F*&# out."*

> *@CharlieBrennabad When you see a punch coming, do you just assume it's going to knock you out?*

Here's another account made strictly to bash me: @CharlieUawake. You gotta give them credit—they are creative and sometimes funny, though NOT when you're laying on your couch concussed from a recently-suffered KO.

I share these with you not to seek your pity or convey that my situation is unique. While I'm not sure the average person has social media accounts created for the mere sake of bashing them, I am 100% sure that the majority of us deal with this type of hate at one point or another. This is part of something I often call A Fighter's Mindset—the fighter knows this, he expects it, it comes with the territory. You are a fighter in this game of life, and you've got to fight tooth and nail not to be swallowed up, and it's all on you.

I'm no stranger to people lovingly rubbing your nose in all that crap that has come your way, whether it's your losses or whatever. People love to hate. You get used to it, and it really doesn't hurt me when haters hate any more. But somebody was hating on my last fight, when I got dropped to the body and making snide comments online. I messaged them, and said, "Thanks, I'm okay," and they pretended like they weren't making snide comments. One thing I said was, "I hope you never have a bad day at the office, like I did. I hope that whatever your bad day at the office is, that it's not in front of thousands of people. I hope that for you, because: Somebody's gonna win, somebody's gonna lose, and the most naked you can be to the world is trying with everything you can, with every weapon in your toolbox, to try to beat this person, and for them to come out on top and hurt you, stop you in front of thousands of people and then it's available for millions of people to see later ... there's no lonelier spot for anyone." I don't wish that on anybody. But I'm so glad that I had that ability to know that feeling. It shows me that I can get through anything, even at the loneliest time.
Justin Greskiewicz
Fighter / Trainer / Owner, Stay Fly Muay Thai
AMXtalks 201

It is not the critic who counts; not the man who points out how the strong man stumbles, or where the doer of deeds could have done them better. The credit belongs to the man who is actually in the arena, whose

face is marred by dust and sweat and blood; who strives valiantly; who errs, who comes short again and again, because there is no effort without error and shortcoming; but who does actually strive to do the deeds; who knows great enthusiasms, the great devotions; who spends himself in a worthy cause; who at the best knows in the end the triumph of high achievement, and who at the worst, if he fails, at least fails while daring greatly, so that his place shall never be with those cold and timid souls who neither know victory nor defeat.
Theodore Roosevelt's words
AMXtalks 18

That's the famous "Man in the Arena" passage. Dread and I covered it on AMXtalks 18. Here are my thoughts on that text now: It's too easy to sit outside the fire and point inward—at the quarterback who threw an interception, the pitcher who gave up a hit, the actor whose movie was a dud—but we do it because it's a natural tendency, and social media serves us the means on a silver platter. Jack Canfield has said that we have 50,000 thoughts a day, and 40,000 are negative (80%). We are wired to be drawn to negativity, so it's got to be an intentional, active process to combat it. I speak first-hand, kicking off 2019 as I write this, to consciously focus on the good rather than the bad.

So how do critics play a role in my life and development? What it boils down to is that ultimately I won't be influenced by them, but in the short-term, I am. My emotions peak and plummet when I see negativity thrown my way. It's the paradox of not caring what anyone thinks about you while also caring what everyone thinks about you.

I will, however, be influenced by people who inspire me. I welcome them with big ol' open arms.

I followed podcasting role models

I know that I already discussed role models, but those are role models I aspire to be like regarding character and ethics. Now I mean role models specific to podcasting and building a business. In some cases, they intersect.

Probably the most influential, long-distance, non-direct "mentorship" that I've received is from Joe Rogan, though he has no idea that we have this relationship. He began podcasting in 2009 kind of by accident, recording with friends, never imagining that *The Joe Rogan Experience* would become one of the most listened-to, talked-about, influential podcasts of all time. I had met and interacted with him during my time in the UFC, enough that he would probably remember my name, but that was basically it. I still cringe at the DM I sent him on Twitter when I released my first book in 2015. Basically, it said, "Hey Joe, I released a book. Can I be a guest on your show?" I had no real sense of reciprocity, nor the abundance of requests he gets on a daily basis. I knew a good bit of his history from watching his TV shows *Talk Radio* and *Fear Factor* in years past, as well as his comedy. What draws me to him is the fact that he has created a successful business—make that many businesses, actually—that revolve around his life. He is himself, and he makes a great living being himself.

I could geek out about the technical aspects of his show, mainly his style of interviewing and how it appeals to me, but in a nutshell, it's his insatiable curiosity and genuine interest, his non-linear / non-predetermined line of questioning, the variety of topics he brings to the show and his differentiation between his ability to remember a lot of information vs. being really smart. He's interviewed hundreds of guests covering a wide variety of topics and is often told that he's very smart. His response is that he's simply good at remembering things. In my own way, I have made a concerted effort to become Joe Rogan. Not in a weird I-want-to-be-a-Kardashian way, but rather also becoming a man who has dedicated a lifetime to acquiring and sharing information with others. In my day-to-day, I can see it happening little by little, thanks in large part to AMX, my system for learning. My notebooks are full of handwritten notes from the books I read, our show notes from interviews are thorough and powerful, and my daily / weekly learning and producing schedule is keeping it fresh in my mind while ingraining it into the fabric of my being. I am becoming, day by day, really... stinking "smart."

My initial thoughts on creating my own podcast

K. I. S. S. —Keep it simple, Stupid. I'm sure my appreciation of simplicity existed before fighting, but it grew along with my fighting career. That whole experience was like the Wild West, so I began to really appreciate and yearn for simplicity—something easy and not stressful. So when Dread and I started the podcast, one of my primary drivers was to make it simple. I always keep these four values in mind when recording: Authenticity, simplicity, quality and quantity. I operate on the idea that I don't want to depend on anyone for anything; not in a sad, depressed, dejected way but in a forward-thinking, objective and efficient way. It's not a foolproof philosophy as no man is an island, but I always keep it in mind when planning and moving forward.

I like the idea of betting on me. Remember that no one in

the world cares more about your success than you do. Let's take Dread, for example. I'm not sure a better partner exists, but if he has a family emergency, and he has to pick between family or Spanny, guess who's playing second fiddle? Of course, as we expand, more and more things will become out of my control, but I'll always do my darnedest to keep it as simple and controllable as possible. Controllable, in the future, will mean creating a solid, dependable team around Dread and me.

To keep the podcast as simple as possible, we decided early on to keep editing to a minimum, if there was any editing at all. My high production rate (producing eight episodes per week) made it a necessity. My aim was / is to marry the least amount of resistance to creating and sharing content with the best possible sound quality within our means at this time. It's a dichotomy—Lean too far one way, and we're taking on additional stress and inhibiting production quality. Lean too far the other way, and our production quality doesn't meet the desired standard for our audience. This is all subjective as the show develops. As we grow, our resources will be greater, our reach further and the desired production level higher. Our norms and standards change in time, but for now, we've found a nice system to consistently and frequently produce a simple, authentic, quality product.

In the beginning, my podcast was just recording talks with Dread. In retrospect, I overshot (still do) how much, and how many, people would care about what I had to say. I had built up a nice following from professional fighting, but it certainly wasn't in the millions, or even hundreds of thousands. In the very beginning, we didn't plan for any interviews, but we also didn't *not* plan for interviews. We weren't thinking that far ahead. We were bootstrapping it, two guys who had no idea what the heck we were doing, thinking that people would care. I got a solid mic (ATR2100), and I already had my MacBook Pro. We went to work.

I just stinkin' started

We created test episodes, me in my attic and Dread in his basement. It's laughable, but it pays tribute to the fact that no one knows what they're doing at the beginning of anything. It's like driving your newborn home from the hospital: What the ... ?! We just went to work, recording the first four episodes in my attic. I had learned that a best practice was to release a batch of episodes at one time to score better on iTunes. The idea, I think, is that iTunes would recognize a bunch of downloads of your show, which would make it "think" we were worthy of being promoted on iTunes by way of its algorithmic something or other. It didn't work, or we did it wrong. Who knows. We launched A Fighter's Mindset on August 9, 2016.

> **A QUICK ASIDE: Dumbness on Day 1**
> (This is Dread speaking) Here's how dumb we were early on: When we first recorded in the same location, we kept trying to record as if we weren't. Our first test podcasts (with each of us in our own house) produced two audio tracks of each conversation, my side and The Spaniard's side, that we combined in GarageBand. It's a common practice called "double enders." When we worked in The Spaniard's attic on the first day of actual recording, it took us hours of experimenting, still trying to produce double-enders, until we realized that when we were together, it would be simplest to record one track by sitting at the same microphone.

Imagine sitting in the same room having a cell phone conversation rather than just talking to each other. That's basically what we were doing at first.

The early days of the podcast

When we started, we didn't have much of a direction, but whatever direction it was, we were moving in it. Our vision for what we wanted to do was our guide: Be a voice and platform to help and inspire people. The ideas of learning and teaching, and the prominent role they would play in the show—those were not yet present. We were simply working off of my experiences, mostly from fighting because that was the little bit of traction, or attention, that I had.

Here are the earliest focus areas and episode titles:

Communication
Nutrition
Mindset
Working out
Relationships
Taking action

(All of these are AMXtalks episodes)
 #1 What is "A Fighter's Mindset"?
 #2 Discovering Desire
 #3 The Two Big Areas of Improvement
 #4 Where Passions Hide
 #5 Tell Me Where I'm Good and Bad
 #6 What Transcends Wins and Losses? Balance
 #7 Take On The Olympian
 #8 The Risk of Not Risking
 #9 But What If You Lose?
#10 An Uncomfortable Working Session

#11 Yes, You Will Still Get Nervous

#12 Speak Up WHEN CONVENIENT?!?

#13 Principles of Fathership

#14 Competing Views of Competition

#15 Get Serious About Having Fun

#16 What Three Fighters Taught Me

#17 One New Step Leads to Another

#18 How to Be "The Man in the Arena"

#19 Unqualified Weight Management Thoughts

#20 How to Speak for 90 Minutes Without Notes

If my superpower is discipline and the ability to work toward a goal without stopping, I was and still am in full superpower mode. I just didn't / don't / won't stop. My mindset is simple, and it goes back to my core values: If I'm authentic, create a lot of great content on a regular basis and keep it simple, I just cannot lose. "Just keep going. Don't stop." I must tell myself a hundred times a day, echoing Phil Knight. We created 200 episodes in six months, initially releasing two episodes per week. In November 2016, I began uploading AMX to my podcast feed. Until that time, AMX lived only on my Facebook page (facebook.com/charliespaniard), and had a brief stint on my Youtube channel (Youtube.com/charliespaniard). We published 600 episodes in the first 18 months and 799 episodes by our second anniversary. And it wasn't about numbers—I had a quality standard that was near obsessive. WE WENT TO WORK. I've heard that the average number of podcasts recorded by new podcasters is something like three. The only way to get past three and then 300, and then 3000, is to grind. The same thing happens with fighters who have the romantic idea of fighting in the UFC. You're all gung-ho about it until you realize how tough and messy the journey really is.

What helps me, and one of the things I got very clear on early, is the reason behind the pursuit of my goals and dreams. It's not really about a #1 podcast, a best-selling book, an international speaking career, a UFC championship, a state title or straight A's, it's about the manifestation of my beliefs and values, and sharing what I view as important. It's about expressing myself to the world, and that never gets tiring. It's about reaching my potential, helping others, working hard, learning and teaching and creating a legacy that will make my kids proud to call me their dad. The path may change, but the mission won't.

7
What Guides Me

PURPOSE

(Quote from Napoleon Hill) The starting point of all achievement is definiteness of purpose.
Phil Jackson
Eleven Rings
AMXbooks 189

When you have something to fight for, the fight is just that much more important.
Joe Lozito
MMA Fan who stopped a spree killer
AMXtalks 76

Find something you'd die for, and give your life to it.
James Kerr
Legacy
AMXbooks 209

We taught our children by both example and instruction, but with emphasis on example.
Kent Nerburn
The Wisdom of the Native Americans
AMXbooks 512

I've said it a bunch of times already in this book, but I could never say it enough. What I want most from writing, speaking, podcasting and all this learning and teaching, is to create a legacy for my kids. I told the story of Gracie's birth in *DRIVEN*, and I told the story of Rocky's birth in lucky episode #13 of the podcast, titled "Principles of Fathership" (including the fact that "Rocky" is his actual given name on his birth certificate). My kids are my North Star. This book is actually for them. You, Reader, are along for the ride.

Parenting is one of those things that falls into "you don't know what you don't know." When we had Gracie, Amanda and I learned quickly what it meant to be a parent. We learned all of the things you can't know unless you're a parent. Of course people advised us, told us what to expect and helped us as much as possible, but until it's just you and your spouse lying in bed, night after sleepless night, exhausted to a level that you didn't even know existed, you can't really know. Another thing you can't know, or even imagine possible, is how your heart can grow so much after your first child, that you can develop that much more available space in your heart for total love and admiration. And when the second child comes, you find even more available space, and your heart grows to a level that totally blows your mind. I suspect this process is the same for child #3, 4 and so on.

But it's hard. Sleep (rest, really) has become a commodity of immense value since having kids. Gracie was a good sleeper. After only a couple months, she was sleeping 8 to 8. Add in everything else people warn first-time parents about, and we figured we had it pretty good. "Meh, this ain't so bad," we thought. Little did we know what was coming our way with baby number 2. While having one baby does indeed have a giant impact on your life, for us it was our second child, Rocky, who really taught us the extremes to which we'd be pushed. I made a Facebook post not long ago and asked, "What's more difficult, going from one to two kids, or from two to three?" The results were surprising. They were split nearly down the middle. All we knew was that we didn't really know anything.

When Gracie was born, I was in the middle of my rebirth in MMA. I had been released from the UFC already and was about to get re-signed. I actually left the hospital a few times to train while Amanda was there, and shortly after Gracie came home I left for New Jersey to resume training. It was a sacrifice, but a necessary sacrifice. When Rocky was born, I was in the early phase of building a business. I was experiencing some personal change, adapting to a life outside of fighting, and it was a very high / low time of my life. One day, something great would happen. The next, I'm sitting in front of my computer aimlessly wandering, asking myself how to make this thing grow. I'm learning daily about new things such as direct marketing and how long it takes to build a business.

An advantage I have in my current set up is that I am home often. I am able to get Gracie and Rocky ready every morning. I am able to visit Gracie at school for off-hour functions when the rest of the world is working. I am able to take them to the doctor when rashes and coughs develop. Or when Rocky stuck a peanut up his nose, and we had to go to a specialist to get it out. (That's a true story. He is almost two and a half.) Though they will most likely not remember the actual moments in which we were together so often at this young age, my belief is that a seed will be planted. They will feel something in them that wouldn't have otherwise been there. They'll have this nudge or twinge inside of them for all time that will let them know, "My dad loves me." They may not even know that the nudge or twinge is there, or if they do, why it's there. But I believe that these little moments will make all the difference. It's the same as the early mornings, late nights and overall sacrifice of the world's best athletes—all of the times that go unnoticed by anyone who's not direct-ly involved.

A QUICK ASIDE: Stitch Duran's parents

I always take note when someone tells me about how their parents shaped them. One example on my pod-cast was my interview with Stitch Duran. Jacob "Stitch" Duran is a "cutman" in professional combat sports. He's written several books, built a successful business off of his craft and has appeared in several big-time movies (Rocky Balboa, Creed, Creed 2, Here Comes the Boom, Ocean's Eleven to name a few). He comes from very humble beginnings and doesn't over-look the importance of his upbringing.

One of my favorite things about Stitch is that he likes being in the trenches, and putting in the work. I asked him where that came from, and here is his reply as captured by Dread in the show notes from AMXtalks 49:

"Growing up, we had no money, but we were given good values, a good work ethic. When workers would come in the summer to pick the crops, a lot of these people didn't have places to stay, didn't have jobs. My mother and father would always get involved with the people coming in and help them out. That was some-thing I blossomed off from my parents. That's the only

thing I knew, was how to give, how to work hard, and how to respect people. That made it easy and gave me the drive. My father was a foreman, so he would hire people, and he had those leader qualities for the position that we were at. Same thing with my mother: She went back to school and got her degree. The Head Start program that you see throughout the United States—she was one of the original people to get that program going. Money doesn't base you, or give you that identity to do things. It's more the ganas *(in Spanish)—the will to go out there and challenge things. I'm not scared of challenging."*

Side note: Stitch mentions Head Start, and Dread was a Head Start kid.

I talk often of my parents and how fortunate I was to be raised by two people who lived their values. I'm sure, at one point or another they explained to me what core values were and maybe even mentioned a few examples, but what we, the Brenneman kids, really saw were two people who lived a certain way, and that way of living influenced us. It started with my oldest brother and trickled down to me. We hear so much about peer pressure in a negative sense, but it can work the opposite way as well. I actually felt compelled to keep up the level of academic and personal performance of my siblings. I was "peer-pressured" in a good way. My close friend, Dave Beard, in his TEDx talk ("It's Not Just What You Say"), describes it as "brainwashing" his kids so that they believe in themselves later in life.

When Dread and I decided to create a podcast, he suggested (paraphrased), "If for the sake of creating, we imagine that no one other than your kids will ever hear these episodes, let that be our guide."

That made all kinds of sense to me, and I continually come back to the idea. It helps me in so many ways. I know why I am creating the show, so no matter how hard it is, how tired I get, how fruitless it seems or how much it feels like treading water and going nowhere, I know there are at least four ears listening. The hilariousness of this all is that Gracie and Rocky may never even listen! They may not even care! If that's the case, I find solace in the fact that they will at least appreciate hearing my voice when I'm gone, my grandkids will know a lot about their grandfather, and the general public will have a resource from which to learn and improve. *The Spaniard Show* is basically saying, "Hey Gracie, Hey Rocky, I love you guys. This is how I lived. I hope you can learn from it and use it to live well and to improve where I lacked. It's a blueprint: This is how you win, this is how you lose, this is how you keep going."

And it's not only telling but showing and doing. As a 38-year-old father of two young kids, I walk an even tighter rope. How could I speak of excellence, resilience, perseverance and so on if I don't actually live it? My kids see me at my best and worst, same as my wife. It's not my perfect track record of living well that will be key, it's the never-ending fire that burns within me and will burn until I'm gone. "In the warrior's code, there's no surrender, though his body says stop, his spirit cries, never." That line from Survivor, from *Rocky*, is as concise as it gets for me. Just. Don't. Stop.

To reinforce this hope for Gracie and Rocky, I've made it a point to expose them to the places where I was taught the warrior's code—the mats and the gym. As I am developing my life, career and future, that consideration is always a front-runner. We've spent many sessions in my makeshift basement gym, giggling on the treadmill, dangling from the boxing bags and swinging enthusiastically from the TRX. Just as Gracie and Rocky will passively learn Spanish through years of consistent repetition, presence and practice, they'll learn the value of hard work through a blend of passive and active consumption.

I'm a very self-reflective person. I consider the ramifications of exposing my kids to my intense and structured lifestyle, but I'm confident that I will lead Gracie and Rocky in the right direction. It doesn't matter to me what they choose to do with their lives, only that it comes from a good place and they're committed to giving it everything they have.

I know that no one can control the outcome of any training or philosophy. In *Unplugged: Evolve from Technology to Upgrade Your Fitness, Performance & Consciousness*, I read a story about Archie Manning and his focus on spending time with his kids after his pro football career. His intent was not to raise his three sons to be Super Bowl champions, it was to spend time with them. He spent time with them in the most natural way he knew: playing football. The result was that two of his three sons (Peyton and Eli) grew up to be Super Bowl champions. The third son, Cooper, who is not in football, is no less successful. *Sports Illustrated* from November 10, 2003 says that Cooper might have had the most potential of the three, but turned out to have a congenital condition that forced him out of contact sports. Archie's intent, my intent, your intent, I believe, is the most important part of the equation.

It's taken maturity and a great deal of strife to recognize, and truly believe, that it's not about the outcome. It's not about making Rocky or Gracie champion athletes, it's about making them champion people by giving them tools to deal with both success and failure. That makes me think of Chris

Cyborg, one of the most dominant women to ever fight in professional combat sports, who, until last week (as of this writing), was the most dominant. After being upset by Amanda Nunes, she wrote on Twitter:

> *Today was not our day, but I want you to know that I am very grateful for your affection! Life is like that. One day we lose and one day we win! Belt for me has always been symbolic, the most important is to be a champion in the lives of people making a difference in the world.*

That, my friends, is what it's truly about.

I find myself stressing "respect" as much as any word when teaching Gracie and Rocky. Just the other day, Gracie came into the kitchen and said, "Dad, I told Rocky respect. People and toys." My heart got all warm and fuzzy. She's taking it in. Respect is all encompassing: People, toys, Earth, yourself. If you grow up respecting yourself and others (as well as your toys, which change in size and dollar value as we grow!), you'll have a solid foundation from which to grow.

I learned very early how important it is to me that my kids respect their mom more than anyone on Earth. I had never had kids, and thus had never seen my child disrespect their mother. That first time stung. Seeing everything Amanda did / does, from the kids' birth to present day, has created an entirely new understanding of a mother's role in her child's life. I'm told I was one heck of a tantrum-thrower as a kid, and I still make mistakes as a son, but understanding how important it is to me that my kids respect their mother influences my actions and the words that come out of my mouth to my own parents—though I admit I have my fair share of 38-year-old temper tantrums.

Another value at the top of the list for my kids is hard work. I absolutely love and believe in hard work, both the actual practice / exercise of it as well as the idea of it. Hard work is good for the soul. It provides a sense of accomplishment. While I'm working hard to provide the best of opportunities for my children, their making the most of those opportunities is contingent on their working hard. They can have the world if they work hard for it, if they earn it.

It's interesting the words or values that become important when raising another human. You just think differently than you did before. Certain things are forgotten, and others are heightened. Regarding respect, Amanda's phrase for the one thing she wants from our kids is a sense of appreciation. The last thing she wants is to raise ungrateful kids who expect things and don't show appreciation. It will be interesting to read this in 10-20 years to see how we did at raising respectful and appreciative kids, and I appreciate the challenge.

Gracie and Rocky are two totally different human beings. Truthfully, I had never envisioned having a girl—something I can't explain. When she was born, it gave me the most purpose I'd ever had in my life. It was now my duty to raise, teach and protect this beautiful little girl and help her develop into a strong and confident woman. She has always had the biggest heart. That a young girl (she's five as I write this) can be so considerate and compassionate blows my mind. She's always been a rule follower and a tremendous big sister. She's a questioner, too. She gets that honestly. (She recently won the Wise Owl Award in her Pre K4 class "For always answering and asking questions!") I have learned very quickly that the areas where I correct her most are the same ones where I was corrected. It gives me pride to see me in her.

Rocky, on the other hand, is straight fire. He is a boy pos-

Gracie echoes Daddy back in the day

sessed. "Relentless Rocky" is a name I used when he was very young. He is not as calm and collected as his sister. We never even felt the need to "baby-proof" our house for Gracie, but with her little brother, the tedious process of screwing in the widgets to keep the cupboards closed was well worth the time. While Rocky is still very young (two and a half as I type), his personality is reflected in his actions. One of my favorite social media posts is side-by-side pictures of Rocky and me. I am at one of my UFC weigh-ins, flexing, jaws open wide, probably letting out a "Raawwrrr!" Next to that photo is Rocky wearing his little red onesie, letting out the same "Raawwrr!"—only he has no idea why. My job with Rocky is

Daddy and Rocky bring the raawwrr

to help curb that intensity, fire and persistence in a positive direction. While it gives me pride to see my characteristics of compassion and curiosity in Gracie, it gives me as much pride to see my intensity and persistence in Rocky. My hope is the same for both—that they use everything Amanda and I teach them to become exactly who they're supposed to be.

8

What Guides Me

AUTHENTICITY

(Quote from Mister Rogers) One of the greatest gifts you can give anybody is the gift of your honest self.
Maxwell King
The Good Neighbor: The Life and Work of Fred Rogers
AMXbooks 138

I always aim to be authentic. I carry my heart on my sleeve. I can't help but express my emotions. I'm a terrible liar, except when I had to lie for reality TV (*Pros vs. Joes*)—for five months following the recording of the show, I couldn't divulge any of the details. If something is wrong with me, you know. In time, I've learned to work with those emotions when it comes to performing in the cage or on stage. It became a necessity to turn them off for a time, but that took lots of practice and many failed attempts. It comes down to simply being myself, embracing all the good and bad that comes with being Charlie Brenneman. Realizing that it's not a fight I have to win, rather the path laid out in front of me.

There are plenty of things I dislike or wish were different about myself. I judge myself on a daily basis, but that's part of the deal. That's part of my drive to be the best in all that I do. Dr. Andy Galpin, Author of *Unplugged*, said on my show (AMXtalks 211):

> *I would say this is all a practice for all of us, so talk to me in a year, and I'll probably tell you I've made another evolution or another step forward in how I do things. I'm just trying to see in the moment and often don't. That's why we call it a practice.*

We're just practicing every day to be our best. I dislike a lot less about me today than I did last year. I'm guessing next year will be even better.

I often talk about how I cheated myself out of wrestling glory by pressing too hard. I lost touch of why I was doing what I was doing. I learned that I had to let go a little in order to move forward, to simplify the sport and everything that went with it. I learned, but I didn't completely learn. At a point well into my UFC career, I began to question myself once again. It wasn't my skill or confidence in my ability to win that wavered, it was that I let others' opinions creep into my mind, and that affected my performance. I began to listen to the critics who criticized my fighting style, labeling me as boring and one-dimensional. Now I know that I am what I am, and I can't control how or what people think, but back then I changed my style to make them happy. The results spoke for themselves. I've paid the price for not being myself and accepting myself, and that is the last thing I want for my kids. I want to model for them the words I often say: Just stinkin' be you. I will always steer my kids to be themselves, and that might make them similar to me and each other, or very different.

This realization and confidence extends outward, far beyond professional fighting or performing. Deep into my fighting career, my buddy Dominick told me, "Man, you're funny. I feel like you've gotten a lot funnier." The confidence I was acquiring, though not absolutely bullet-proof, had elevated my personality in other areas of my life. And it will yours, too. But you've got to work for it. And you've got to commit to never stop working for it. I still fight daily to put that doubt and negativity in the corner with Baby.

Here are ways that I am authentic on screen / stage and off: I speak from my core, non-scripted. I carry my heart on my sleeve. I express myself. I present my story and material from books in a completely vulnerable way. My mindset is: I am Charlie. I am learning. I am sharing what I learn and what I've done. I am not exactly sure what I will think of all of this in time, but here and now this is who I am and what I think. It may change, so please don't hate me if it does. I'm in this to learn, and sometimes that means I'll change. I always aim to be authentic, and I would say I hit the target a great deal of the time. It's easy to be authentic if you commit to being yourself, to listening to you instead of them. Just produce clear, direct, honest communication.

Podcast me is just me

I am simply myself on the podcast. That might sound obvious, but you can be phony without realizing it. Soon after I started the show, Amanda came to point out when I was using my "podcast / speaking voice". That voice was coming out when I was lecturing or posturing. I was being something I wasn't. Rather than speaking clearly to the audience, my podcast voice goes like this: (1) Words are formulated in my brain and began to descend to my mouth. (2) When the words are right around my nose, between my brain and mouth, I ask myself, "What will they think if I say these words?" (3) Static is created. Communication becomes non-direct. (4) If I deem it necessary, I alter the words a bit. If not, they come out of my mouth as is. (5) As a result of this mumbo-jumbo, I sound like a tool. I realized after the fact where it came from: I thought I had to be smarter / better / different / more profound than I really am, or people wouldn't listen to me. It was already important to me to be myself, but that was a specific lesson in HOW to be myself.

I'll caveat this with something Diamond Dallas Page (AMXtalks 111) told me on my show. He explained that The Rock, Stone Cold or DDP that we see in the WWE are expansions of who they are in real life. They amp it up for the camera. They're able to remain uniquely themselves while being "turned up," a term that former guest and pro wrestler Mike "Cowboy Gator Magraw" Kinney (AMXtalks 136) explains in his TED Talk "A Pro Wrestler's Guide to Confidence." (Google it. Watch it.) On camera and on stage, I speak with more energy than I do in my daily life, but I strive with every opportunity to speak clearly and directly from my heart.

I've developed my own approach as a speaker

I am not pre-packaged on stage, and that fits perfectly with my personality, or maybe because of my personality. I get bored really easily. I need spice in my life. I need variety.

I did experiment with one potential formula on my show. AMXtalks 161 showcased "The Five Finger Fist of Success":

- Learning
- Implementing the Learning
- Putting in the Time
- Building Skill
- Luck

It went nowhere, but it served its purpose. Really, it was a test, molding some ideas into a cohesive, reproducible thing, and seeing if it took off. It did not take off, but it does still make a lot of sense. And the meta lesson is that that's the game right there: Try, fail, try again, fail again, repeat as many times as necessary until you don't fail. Wait, did I just create another fist of success?!

Instead of using a formula on stage, my approach is: Tell my story up to the minute; it's ever-evolving and changing and will continue to do so. If I am to be the World's Toughest Lifelong Learner, I must continue to be the World's Toughest Lifelong Learner. At this point, my story is:

- Wrestler
- Teacher
- Reality show winner
- Fighter
- Author
- WTLL
- Always learning

Within that framework, I share my learnings, both those that are current, those that are staples, and those that are specific to my audience.

Just stinkin' be you. This is the story of Ferdinand.
Munro Leaf
The Story of Ferdinand
AMXkids 17

I talk about my true heroes

It does feel a little weird to use the word "hero" as a grown man, but, honestly, I can't think of a better word. Add the fact that, at age 38, I'm still a kid with big dreams and goals, and it fits. I suppose, in reference to Rocky Balboa and The Rock, I could say "person I'd like to be like" or "person whose characteristics I admire and respect," but hero just sounds better.

Mythologist Joseph Campbell described what he called "The Hero's Journey." In his words:

> *A hero ventures forth from the world of common day into a region of supernatural wonder: fabulous forces are there encountered and a decisive victory is won: the hero comes back from this mysterious adventure with the power to bestow boons on his fellow man.*

Rocky Balboa has been my own Hero's Journey since I was young.

I find the height of humanity in Rocky and the Rock. They represent a very simple idea that comes across in their beings. It's a message of hard work, sweat, belief, adversity, humility, perseverance and serving as a role model / point of hope to others. They are everything I want to be. Inherent in their beings are certainly flaws, but it's not the flaws I'm focusing on. I'm sure Adrian had to put up with her fair share of Rocky's shenanigans, and I'm sure The Rock is not always the hero at his house, but that's real, and reality is what I'm a fan of. It has tremendous power, like so:

> *(Quote from Vince Lombardi) Perfection is unattainable, but if we chase perfection, we just might catch excellence.*
> **David Maraniss**
> **When Pride Still Mattered**
> **AMXbooks 242**

Having said that, I have my heroes in a proper place. I don't need them to actually be perfect. I only need to cling to the pieces of them that fuel my fire. I could make this journey on my own, without fuel from others, but why would I? It's much more fun admiring the hard work of others and seeking to emulate it. I'm not a 10-year-old whose heart will be crushed if I find out my heroes aren't perfect. I know that perfection is not only unattainable for me, but for anyone.

> *Anybody who is your hero, who you think never slips up—that is just not true. They are Just. Like. You.*
> **Adee Cazayoux**
> **CEO/Founder of Working Against Gravity**
> **AMXtalks 139**

> *Scott Adams finds it "helpful to remind myself that every human is a mess on the inside."*
> **Scott Adams**
> **How to Fail at Almost Everything and Still Win Big**
> **AMXbooks 361**

You can't be yourself without letting others, even your heroes, be themselves, and that means being imperfect. I do my best to look for the good in people and things. I recognize that Rocky Balboa is a fictional slice of humanity. I know that he represents an ideal and only an ideal, but I also know that George Pocock, boat builder and mentor to the 1936 Olympic Gold Medal Men's Rowing Team (*The Boys in the Boat*) conducted himself in "a lifelong pursuit of the ideal." I, too, believe in this lifelong pursuit, and I dedicate my life to it. And I know that it is the same with The Rock, because I don't see all that there is to see about him. How he and his family work out the fact that he travels for months at a time, I do not know, but I do know that it takes working it out. Perfectly smooth and seamless is an ideal only, but it's one worth fighting for. The Rock has shared his flaws and mistakes in interviews. Note: One place he does this is in the *SuperSoul Conversations* podcast from Oprah.

If I "worship" these heroes, it is in that context. I'm doing it with an awareness of reality. I recognize them as admirable but authentic beings, which is my whole point in this chapter. And I don't need myself to be perfect either. I may have needed that one day long ago, but when you get your butt kicked and KO'd on live television, the secret is out of the bag: That guy ain't perfect.

I don't hide my imperfections

An easy and fun example of accepting my own imperfections is the fact that Spaniardisms are a thing, albeit within a small community. Those are when I frequently substitute one word for another or invent a new one. Earlier, I mentioned "Uncomfortability." I have a theory that these actually come from having learned Spanish as a second language. A common practice by people who speak Spanish and English is Spanglish, or the combining of pieces of words / phrases / ideas from each language to form a new word / phrase that is neither English nor Spanish, nor actually, technically, a word. However, it becomes a word through usage. The idea, to me anyway, is that it's easier to combine a piece of this English word and a piece of that Spanish word to convey what I want to convey, rather than speaking correct grammar in either, or both, languages. It's laziness, maybe, or our brain's natural tendency to simplify and make easier. My familiarity with Spanglish and creating new words and ideas has triggered me to follow that process in English-only speaking. Examples: To me, "uncomfortability" is easier to understand and more useful than the real word "discomfort." To me, "summate" makes more sense than "summarize" It's also shorter and easy to say. AND you get the point. (By the way, "summate" was a word that Scott Adams called me out for, in a fun way, when I interviewed him.)

It's taken almost 30 years, but, overall, I'm not bothered when I fall short. More precisely, if I am bothered I don't let the bothered-ness keep me from moving forward.

I fall short every day as a / an:

Husband
Father
Son
Brother
Business person
Podcaster
Author

… but because I know that I'm doing my best, I'm okay with it. What I mean is that I'm not bothered in the long term. In the short term, I feel awful. I beat myself up daily, but I've gotten better at getting past embarrassment or disappointment in myself. One of the things that has helped me most is talking. Dread helps me with this. He's as much my therapist as partner. He reminds me about trajectory—the pattern over time versus the current point. It's called course correction. Make it a point to regularly come back to the present to discuss and assess so that you never get too far off course.

9

What Guides Me

HUMILITY

Get over that idea that you're flawless, that you don't make mistakes. Once you come to grips with: "You know what? I'm going to go as hard as I can in the opposite direction. All I'm going to do is try to reveal all my flaws, all my mistakes, all my errors. I'm going to own all those and share those with everybody else around me." That's TOPGUN in a nutshell.

Dave Berke
Retired Marine Corps Fighter Pilot
and TOPGUN Instructor
Leadership Instructor, Echelon Front
AMXtalks 117

I value lessons from failure, and it's taken lots of work and experience to truly appreciate them. When you break down success in any sense, you will see a long line of failures in its wake. No one—NO ONE—gets to the top of the mountain without having failed along the way. "Fail forward" is an idea you should cement on your brain.

I value humility, especially after having spent close to a decade interacting with the world's best while fighting, and seeing how much they practice and value it. How often have you felt the pressure to keep up or fit in? Me? Often. And I remember the relief I felt those times when someone broke the ice and let me know that it was okay to be scared or tired or confused and that I didn't have to have it all figured out. Most often, this person was at the top of their game, the best of the best. It shone a light into their world, exposing that even at the top there still exist fears and anxieties that plague us regular folk down below.

Just as it connected me to these superstars, humility will help people connect to you, because they find themselves in you. As I write this, I'm reading *American Wife* by Taya Kyle, wife of the late Chris Kyle, the U.S. Military's most proficient sniper and author/subject of the book and film *American Sniper*. She stated directly how Chris's humility is what drew people to him—that they saw themselves and their stories in him. Don't underestimate how your humility can positively affect those around you. It gives them hope to know that they don't have to be perfect to succeed. Reading *American Wife*, you will see that same humility echoed in Taya.

> *When you go out there and you suck at something, it's humbling, but if you keep after it, it keeps your creative juices flowing. I find the more you do stuff like that, the more people gravitate toward you.*
> **Matt Furman**
> **Elite Photographer (and fellow Hollidaysburger)**
> **AMXtalks 134**

Senator Bill Bradley (former NBA player) kept a framed picture of himself missing a game-winning shot in the conference finals. He did it to remind himself of his own fallibility.
Phil Jackson
Eleven Rings
AMXbooks 187

The foremost requirement for potent leadership is humility.
Jocko Willink / Leif Babin
The Dichotomy of Leadership
AMXbooks 583

Every combat leader must be humble or get humbled. We knew that being humbled in training was infinitely better than being humbled on the battlefield.
Jocko Willink / Leif Babin
The Dichotomy of Leadership
AMXbooks 589

I've learned what is NOT necessary after honest mistakes or falling short despite giving it your all: Shame and embarrassment. It's a common tendency, and one that I still fight to this day, but think about it: All you can do is all you can do. We are what we are. If you can buy into this and distance yourself from shame and embarrassment after falling short, you'll save that much more time and energy—time and energy that can be spent productively pursuing the things most important in your life. At this point in my life and career, I haven't mastered the emotional game. I still have daily emotional ups and downs. The look on my face can give a good idea of the day I had or the prospects on the table. In time, my ideal is such that a good day or a bad day will be indecipherable from the look on my face.

That one skill—to not feel shame or embarrassment about things that frankly other people don't care about, because they have their own problems ... as soon as you get that out of your head, you're free.
Scott Adams
Creator of "Dilbert"
AMXtalks 144

Josh Waitzkin speaks of "the importance of regaining presence and clarity of mind after making a serious error" as a vital component of consistently high performers.
Josh Waitzkin
The Art of Learning
AMXbooks 492

When you're learning a foreign language, it's just like fighting. At first, YOU WILL STINK. There's no other way around it. You can't fake it. You just gotta start.
Speak Spanish with Spaniard 1

I either correct the mistakes that I can recognize, or I do my darnedest to correct them. I'm writing this the day after I gave a talk at a STE(A)M middle school in Harrisburg PA, and in an effort to give my best self, I repeated to myself before I started, "It's not about you. It's about them. It's about the books. Just be yourself." I repeated this mantra because, at times, I do make it about me. I get nervous that I'll mess up or feel like an idiot on stage. I forget that it's not about me, it's about the mission. It's about spreading the value of lifelong learning and the power of perseverance. It's about being a good person, about inspiring empathy and positivity in young people. On that day, this little mantra helped keep me centered and helped me deliver a kickbutt performance. I recognized a mistake / tendency, and I course-corrected it.

Some other focus areas: Not using my "speaking" voice, creating better transitions and segues on AMXbooks, avoiding using filler words like "umm" and "ahh," controlling the speed at which I deliver my message, deliberately including pauses to let a point sink in, and varying the tone of my voice (serious / joking and so on).

10

ENERGY

There are at least two ways of doing business: (1) Identify a problem / challenge / point of difficulty in society and solve it by way of a product or service, or (2) Be you, create what feels right and true, with no guarantee or consideration of an audience / clientele who cares, and keep on keeping on out of nothing but belief in the purity of what you do. Right or wrong, I gravitate toward #2. I have to do what excites and interests me, or I will be a shell of myself.

Johnny Waite knows energy

When it comes to following your area of energy, Johnny Waite (AMXtalks 133) put it as simply and awesomely as I have ever heard it put. I had ventured out to Lake Tahoe, California for the Spartan Race World Championships as part of a "podcast fest," an opportunity from the Spartan brand, which invited select podcasters to the world championships to interview some extraordinary people who were in Lake Tahoe for the event. One of the remarkable people I sat down with was Johnny Waite, one of the hosts of the *Spartan Up!*

podcast. I didn't know much about Johnny, other than his very noticeable voice from the podcast. He has one of those voices that just sticks out. I've been told that people immediately recognize him when they hear his voice: "Hey, you're Johnny Waite from the *Spartan Up!* podcast."

I felt Johnny's energy from the moment we sat down. He immediately made me think of Ted Turner, whose charisma and energy I had recently read about in *Call Me Ted*. Otherwise, all I knew about him was his voice from the podcast and (based on his bio in the podfest guest list) that his experiences include "surviving a blizzard on one of the highest mountains in the world, dodging gunfire in one of the deepest canyons, eloping on a bicycle built for two in Argentina and surfing in his home-away-from-home in Nicaragua." Those few sentences stirred up a great deal of questions and curiosity. To be honest, that's my favorite way to orchestrate conversations—as if we'd just met and had the opportunity to learn about / from each other.

Johnny had a great deal of knowledge, wisdom and experience to share with me, but perhaps the most notable soundbite I took from our conversation was "a lifetime of adventures of a lifetime." It's his motto, and even a tattoo on his arm. On my podcast, he expanded on it:

> *People will do something and go, 'It was the adventure of a lifetime.' And I think, 'Really? You gonna mail it in now?' I've been really fortunate to have a lot of incredible experiences, and I find that one cascades into another. Every time you say yes to something, it opens up another door. Why not design your life so that it's an adventure in itself that just keeps getting more and more interesting?*

That is what I have tried to do. Through professional fighting, I learned that people develop a strong connection with other people who put all of themselves into the pursuit of something. That pursuit doesn't have to be extraordinary or superhuman, either. It just has to be pure and whole. We respect and admire that piece of another person that is often not present in ourselves, though we wish it were. We all want to be free, unhindered by fear and self-doubt, to be our truest, most honest selves, but very few of us have the courage to be just that. We see it as too impossible a task.

When I set out to pursue the UFC, I had no idea of the effect it would have on other people. I didn't know how rare it was to go after something you want. I was simply doing what I do and have always done. The ripple effect it had on other people was a bonus that started to show its face after the initial "What in the heck are you doing?" phase. I learned very quickly that most people just don't do that. It's not normal. There is a big discrepancy that exists for most people between who they are and who they want to be. I don't understand that. I've always dealt with self-doubt, more so than the average person, I'd surmise, but it never kept me from acting, from doing. Sure, my self-doubt would cause me to crumble under the lights at times, but I never ran from the lights.

As my fighting career evolved, I began to receive more and more messages and comments that were showing me how my pursuit of being the best in the world was having a powerful effect on the people around me, near and far. Post-fighting, I decided to bottle that effect on people and devise a way to document the next big "something" in my life. I imagined how valuable and rich for people it would have been if I had documented the entire process from deciding to leave my Spanish teaching position to getting choked out in Brazil in November, 2014 (my last fight). As I pursue the bold task of placing The Spaniard in the same sentence as great performers and communicators like Tony Robbins and Joe Rogan, I'm showing the process, by way of audio and video, from start to finish. I'm still fearful, but the self-doubt has been whittled away for the most part. My purpose is to show you that it can be done.

How a particular energy led me to produce AMXkids

My love of learning is what has shaped my podcast and speaking, and a special enthusiasm within all of that lies in AMXkids. I've always had a passion for helping kids, for providing encouragement and support, for offering hope and belief in themselves, and in doing the right thing. Combining that passion with the model set forth by one of my long-distance virtual role models, Jocko Willink, who added "Warrior Kids" as a second podcast (Jocko Podcast being the first), I decided to start a kids track on *The Spaniard Show*. AMXkids is where I talk about the lessons in kids' books.

There are several reasons why AMXkids might not seem to make sense. I began to do these episodes with the intention of speaking to kids. My tone, message and word usage are directed at kids. In time, however, Dread and I realized that probably very few kids are listening to the show. Our gut sense is that it's adults who are listening, adults who've grown to appreciate rekindling the "kid" inside of them by listening to the lessons in these kids' books.

My hope is that AMXkids will be picked up by teachers as a regular classroom instructional aid. The AMXkids episodes are actually longer than my AMXbooks episodes.

There's no predetermined reason, they just are. Another irony is simply that a professional fighter is so stinkin' pumped to dive into these kids books and teach their lessons. I freely admit that you can point to lots of things about AMXkids that you could say don't make sense.

But it just works. I never feel more like myself than when I am AMX'ing a book, and to do so in an effort to help and encourage young people makes it even more special. Nothing feels more exciting or important to me. When I'm recording AMXkids, I'm talking to my kids (who hopefully will listen one day), kids in general, adults and oddly enough, to myself when I was a kid. It's almost a kind of therapy.

AMXkids grew out of a number of things: My identification with kids who are going through challenging times and experiences. Nostalgia for that time in my own life, and the difficulties of facing my own challenges with bullies and making sense of the world, and the part of me that will always remain a teacher. From 2004-2007, as a Spanish teacher, I would tell my students that I was a teacher of life with a specialty in Spanish. Now, I'm simply a teacher of life.

I found a rightness in talking to kids who aren't there, parallel to how Mister Rogers addressed kids directly. It doesn't matter to me if a kid is actually listening, because I believe that by putting that message out into the universe, its energy will connect with a kid who needs it, just when he or she needs it. I believe that the force of AMXkids and the hope and belief that it offers will create a frequency of good that will be received by a young person who needs it; maybe they'll never even know the source of that boost to keep on keeping on.

Hey, you, kid ... I mean, Hello Reader who might have a kid or know a kid. Could you please pass AMXKids on to them? It'll teach them character development, leadership and doing the right thing through books.
AMXkids 3

11
What Guides Me

BOLDNESS

Marco Polo once said, "The bold may not live forever, but the timid do not live at all."
Dean Karnazes
The Road to Sparta
AMXbooks 293

BOLD is a word that developed organically to summarize The Spaniard. Dread, with whom I'm always conversing and exchanging ideas, brought it to my attention. From his perspective, I live with a bold mindset. He views the things I do as bold. I like the idea because it represents a battle I've had with myself since I was old enough to create the battle in my head. Bold means confident and courageous, but am I really confident and courageous?

The truth is I am, and I am not. I've always been confident and courageous, but I've also nearly always lacked confidence and courage. It is / was the paradox within me, "the paradox that drives us all" (Survivor, "Burning Heart," *Rocky IV*) that keeps me battling with myself. Who will wear the crown? Confidence or doubt? After many years of trial and error, happy times and sad times and total exhaustion from trying so hard, I finally decided that I, confident Charlie, was going to win. I stopped thinking and went to work. I worked so hard, so insanely consistently and disciplined, that there was no real room for the self-doubt to settle within me. As soon as it would show its ugly face, I would hop on the treadmill, go to the gym, read a book, listen to an interview or engage in a good conversation to quiet that persistent foe.

Boldness is learnable. Sure, some people are born "fearless" or naturally have less inhibition than the average person, but I do believe, from my own journey, that we have the ability to develop boldness. It's a choice. The tagline for my show when it was called Spaniard101 was "Learn to Be Bold" because I truly believe that. The more you know, the more confident you will be. You can always fight the battle of knowledge, which means you can always learn that thing that will keep you moving forward. Fighting is a lot less scary when you actually learn the techniques that make up the sport / practice of fighting. Tests are much less intimidating when you've studied your butt off. Pitching your business becomes much less daunting after you've done it a hundred times and feel comfortable with your product. I'm not just talking about feeling determined or pumped up, though that is good. I'm talking about a level of preparation that directly corresponds to confidence and boldness. I mean using your brain to absorb information and enhance your level of being. When you know, you walk taller. If it makes it more clear, shuffle the words and say it this way: To Be Bold, Learn.

At one point the title of this book was *Learn to Be Bold*, emphasis on LEARN. It wasn't going to be called *Be Bold*, as I had initially suggested. Dread made the argument that this whole thing is about LEARNING to be Bold. It's about taking someone who's not bold and giving them the tools to become bold. That made total sense. My vision quest in life is rooted in the desire to become bold, to live confidently and coura-geously.

Boldness can be learned and taught, and now I'm out to teach it. By definition, to teach means to "impart knowledge, to guide the studies of," so it is my objective to impart the knowledge of those who live boldly and to guide your study of becoming bold yourself. It's extremely important to fully understand and buy into the fact that you can learn to be-come bold, just as I did, and still am. Boldness is a controllable that YOU control.

I'm purposely putting myself in a corner, because that's the message I want to teach you. That's the kick in the butt I want to give you. I'm putting myself into a corner saying: Watch. Just watch. This or that may not work. So what? I'm moving forward. Come hell or high water, it's gonna work. That's the boldness, those are the cojones that I want you to have in your everyday life.
AMXtalks 97

One way to be bold is to ASK

Success Principle #17 - Ask! Ask! Ask!
Jack Canfield
The Success Principles
AMXbooks 427

One secret behind this podcast is lots of asking. Jack Canfield even suggests that you become an "Askhole" in his Success Principle "Ask! Ask! Ask!" How cool, fun and true is

that? You want something? You have to go and get it! If
you're anything like me, you've thought, "Oh, I've already
called them. I don't want to reach out again. I don't want
them to get upset with me." Yes, you can be an annoying
bother if you take it too far, but you also have to come to rec-
oncile the fact that people are busy, they have a million
things going on, you are not their top priority, and it's partly a
game of chance that you're playing. It's a nuanced game, and
you'll decide when it's time to move on. All you can do is be
sure you're doing it with the right intent, and be as kind as
possible. I'm still learning this idea to this day, on phone calls I
actually made the morning I wrote this. I need to believe I
have a great product that will help this group of people. I will
push, with respect, until they say "No."

> *You've got to ask for what you want in life. You can't
> just wait for things to happen. I think we have this nat-
> ural tendency to be fearful of asking for things in life.
> What's the real downside?*
> **Max Major**
> **World-Renowned Mentalist**
> **AMXtalks 77**

> *Asking for people's help—rather than directing it—is
> almost always the smart way of doing things.*
> **Brian Grazer**
> **A Curious Mind**
> **AMXbooks 501**

Asking is a tricky thing, one that must be balanced. I'm
sure you all know that guy or girl who, at the sound of their
name, you want to run away. "Noooooo! I don't want any!!!" I
ask people to visit my website and connect on social media. I

ask for letters of reference. I ask people to leave reviews on Amazon and iTunes. I used to have a romantic vision that things will just work, that people will simply love my content so much that they will need no urging to follow through on the aforementioned actions. They will read my book and jump to Amazon immediately to leave a review. They will shout my name and proclaim my speaking acumen just as Ralphie from *A Christmas Story* proclaims the glory of the Red Rider BB Gun. They will tell the world that *The Spaniard Show* is the best show on Earth with no prompting whatsoever. Truth is, they may, but they probably won't. Growing my business is my focus, not theirs. I'm thinking from my perspective, not theirs. I'm learning to replace the romantic idea of easy growth with the proper amount of asking.

Asking got me great guests

One of the coolest outcomes of asking has been the incredibly eclectic group of guests who I've had on my show. I literally read a book, watch a movie / documentary or see a thing and think, "Dang, I'd like to talk to that person." Then I ask. I find the person on social media or some other manner of connection, and I ask. Many attempts have been lost in the ether, but many others have been answered. Some of the best examples are:

Diamond Dallas Page, AMXtalks 111
Marc Mero, AMXtalks 152

I got DDP's email through a fellow podcaster and asked if he'd send a Happy Birthday shoutout to my friend / client Dave, a guy who'd lost over 100 pounds by way of hard work (including DDP Yoga) and was a super fan. DDP responded with great kindness, inviting us to his brother's house in NJ to record an episode. This relationship led to my friendship with Marc Mero (WWE star / America's #1 School Presenter). Marc and I still talk regularly, and he serves as a big mentor in my speaking career.

Scott Adams, Creator of "Dilbert"
AMXtalks 144

I read *How to Fail at Almost Everything and Still Win Big* and was captivated. The creator of Dilbert had a new fan. I reached out cold, and he responded. Two people from different planets connecting to create a lasting experience.

Fred "Chico" Lager, Former CEO, Ben & Jerry's,
AMXtalks 74

I read *Ben & Jerry's: The Inside Scoop* (the history of the company) and HAND-WROTE the author a letter! I couldn't find any online connection, so I took to some old-school detective work and mailed him PAPER. The connection we formed is one I'll remember forever.

Richard Turner, World's Best Card Mechanic,
AMXtalks 176

You want to watch an incredible documentary? Look no further than *Dealt*. Richard Turner's story is awesome! I saw his documentary and needed to talk to him. (P.S. You'll find a twist to this story you never expected).

Chris Voss, Former Lead FBI Hostage Negotiator,
AMXtalks 146

What a super experience this was. I read Chris's book on negotiation, *Never Split the Difference*, and saw the challenge in front of me. How do I get this guy to talk to me?! Well, turns out I just had to ask. Such a cool guy with a master skillset.

Joe De Sena, Founder of Spartan
AMXtalks 70

I approached Joe De Sena with wide eyes and an open mind. I saw him as a man who has succeeded in creating a world-class brand, and I wanted to learn from him. He was part of my vision. After reaching out to (pestering) the *Spartan Up!* podcast for a few months on Twitter, I finally connected with Marion Abrams, the podcast producer. She connected me with Joe, and we exchanged a few emails. He mentioned the upcoming 2016 Spartan Wrestling Camp and asked if I would like to be a part of it. "YES!" But then I thought, "The trip to Vermont is a long one. What about money? Should I ask to get paid? Should I do it for free? I'll be away from my family for several days, AND my wife is pregnant."

Patience is a virtue, and it's never been a strong suit of mine. Impulse, on the other hand, has always been, well, on hand. I've had to add fuel to my patience fire and put water on my impulse fire. How that worked in this case is: Rather than firing off an email asking to get paid, I paused. I thought about the end goal, the vision of where I wanted to go. Joe De Sena's influence, small or large, would be invaluable. I nervously typed, "Sure, I'd love to. Do you think it would be possible to cover travel to and from Vermont?" (without any mention of getting paid for the camp.) If he would have said no, I would have gone anyway, but I figured I would ask.

In the end, he said yes, but what I later found out is the entire reason I'm telling you this story. In as many words, Joe later said to me, "You know what stuck out about you? You didn't ask for money. Most people come with their hands out, but you didn't."

That lesson has stuck with me as much as anything. Don't get me wrong, there's certainly a time and place to ask for money and / or to do things for free, but it's up to you to seek out advice and gain experience so that you can tread that water as well as possible when the time comes. I know I've messed it up on other occasions, but you can only live and learn.

Dave Berke, Former Marine Corps Fighter Pilot and TOPGUN Instructor AMXtalks 117

Early in my transition from professional fighter to professional speaker, I came across Jocko Willink. As I've already mentioned, Jocko is a former Navy SEAL who co-authored a book with fellow SEAL Leif Babin called *Extreme Ownership*. It's a book every one of you should read. When I came across Jocko, he was doing the podcast rounds on some of the biggest shows out there. I first caught him on *The Tim Ferriss Show* and *The Joe Rogan Experience*. I was immediately drawn to him and his ideals. He's a tough dude with a no-nonsense approach to leadership. I knew early he was someone from whom I wanted to learn, so I bought the book, read it, followed him on social media and opened my mind to the Extreme Ownership philosophy, which aligned closely with my Element of Excellence 4: Accountability.

What I did next took a bit of gumption, but it was easy, really: I reached out to Jocko. I asked him to be on my podcast. I was overshooting my logical target here, but I am okay with overshooting a target. It turned out to be a pretty good idea for a normal kid from normal Hollidaysburg, PA, to over-shoot his target in professional fighting. I was simply repeat-ing the process. I want to reiterate and spell out the learning principle there: Reach out. Ask questions. Talk to people. Take initiative. If you never ask, you'll never know.

The story didn't turn out how you might think it might have, and that's exactly why I'm telling it. After six months of friendly emails with one of Jocko's team, I was told Jocko was still extremely busy, but she would put me in direct contact with two of his partners who were willing and available to talk. That's how I met Dave Berke, retired Marine Corps fighter pilot and TOPGUN instructor and team member of Echelon Front, Jocko and Leif's leadership consulting compa-ny. My objective was simple: Talk with Dave and share his story so we could all learn from his life experiences. He invit-ed me to his house to make it happen.

I left with simple advice from my brother: "Do not men-tion *Top Gun!*" (the movie) He was concerned my fanboy-ness would get in the way of a good conversation, but I was will-ing to risk it. I ran different scenarios with my wife on how I should end the interview, which movie quotes I should use where, and how I should incorporate "Danger Zone" into the episode. Prior to recording, I had found out about Dave's new-found interest in jiu-jitsu, so we doubled up on my trip down and did some BJJ prior to recording. It turned out to be a per-fect combination.

The episode is gold from start to finish. Famous author Napoleon Hill talks about practical dreamers, people who dream, but who dream practically, as in (my words), "I will systematically chase down this dream by doing x, y and z." Dave Berke is a practical dreamer, saying this on the episode:

*By 16, I was 100% committed to wanting to fly air-
planes for the Marine Corps. I knew exactly what I
wanted to do, exactly how I wanted to do it, where I
wanted to be stationed. I even knew what squadrons I
wanted to be in. It became a practical thing: "This is
something someone is gonna do." I decided I was
gonna do it.*

Sometimes, it's that easy. You just know, and you just do.
There's obviously no guarantees with anything, but Dave
Berke was committed to his dream and was willing to put in
the work to make it come to fruition. "Spend less time dream-
ing about it," he said, "and more time being practical about it."
What dream are you setting for yourself, and how will you
practically achieve it? Those two sides need to match up.

I honestly don't know why guests of this caliber give me
the time of day, but if I had to put it into a lesson for you to
follow, I'd say humility and curiosity have served me the
best. The humility comes from being raised a certain way
and getting my a** kicked on LIVE television, and the curiosity comes from my natural love of learning and asking questions. When you're genuinely interested in learning something from someone for the sake of learning, there's magic.

A QUICK ASIDE: Leif Babin

*Just one more thought related to Echelon Front. Since
I first started this book, Leif Babin, co-founder and
President/COO of Echelon Front, has become a unique
friend and mentor. He's gone out of his way to offer
advice, answer questions and spend time with me on
the phone. When I think of Leif, I think values. He's got
a strong bond with his wife and kids, and he serves as
a role model to me as I develop in life and business.
Success can alter your view on what's really important*

*in life, so it's nice to see Leif handle business and life
as he does. I'm fortunate to have met and become
friends with him.*

ANOTHER QUICK ASIDE: Mike Ritland
*With all this talk of military / Navy SEALs / leadership,
I'd be remiss if I didn't mention my experience with
Mike Ritland (AMXtalks 172). He is a former Navy
SEAL canine trainer who now trains dogs for service,
security, military and police duty, as well as family
pets. As a dog lover and leadership connoisseur, I find
it fascinating how he connects leading dogs to leading
people. I highly recommend his book* Team Dog *and
his podcast* Mike Drop. *I even joined his online training
program to teach my old French bulldog Josie new
tricks, and for sure it has helped me understand her
perspective.*

12

TAKING ACTION

How The Podcast Has Developed

Dread and I started podcasting and have never stopped. As I say over and over, quoting Phil Knight: "Just keep going. Don't stop." It's a great time to be in business from a technology standpoint. I certainly didn't get into the podcasting game at its beginning, but it's still new, and I still come across people who've never heard of a podcast, much less listened to one. It's relatively easy to capture recordings and distribute them, which fits perfectly with the value I place on simplicity. Of course, it's easy for everyone else as well, so there are a lot of other podcasts vying for attention.

I thought through the new competition I was in

I don't like losing. When I lost my second state wrestling title in a row in 1999, I was searching for the perfect vanity license plate. Two quick asides: (1) I come from a family of vanity license platers and (2) Is there such a thing as a perfect vanity plate?!? I came up with "2xsilvr" (On top of this, my AOL screen name back in the day was c2xsilvr, with the "C" for "Charlie."). It made sense and fit the guidelines of a PA license plate. I asked my inner circle for some input before finalizing the plate, and a close friend suggested "2xloser". Obviously, he was joking, but there was a nugget of truth in his reasoning. Not until many years later did I perceive my two runner-up finishes at the PIAA (Pennsylvania Interscholastic Athletic Association) Wrestling Championships as any part of good. The medals were a constant reminder of the failures that I experienced, and, in essence, the loser that I was. That mindset led me into a college wrestling career that felt 75% loser-ish, and 25% winner-ish, even though I won nearly twice as many matches as I lost. It was that 25% that led me to where I am today, and it was a simple mindset shift that was the cause. Losing just eats at me.

As a high-achieving, purpose-DRIVEN person, there are two elements simultaneously at work in my belly: (1) The desire to be the best in the world and (2) The desire to be my own personal best. I still haven't quite put my finger on the perfect mix of the two, but I'm certain they are both extremely important pieces of the puzzle. For much of my life, I had a success mindset that I believe is common to the average person: Win=Success, Lose=Failure. Only through experience has that mindset changed.

There's a lot of talk and debate over doing the best you can versus winning. I WANT TO WIN in everything I do. I want this book to be a best-seller and reach millions and millions of people. There's no way around it. I'm a competitor, and competitors want to win. Winning in that sense means my hand being raised at the end of the match.

Through experience, years of winning and losing, I've learned that winning means a lot more than just having your hand raised. In time, the games, fights and matches came to an end. Then it was just me and the guy I saw brushing my teeth in the mirror every night. I had to learn to be okay with that guy. That's really what winning is: Being okay with the man or woman you see staring back at you in the mirror.

So here is what I think of the podcaster who I see in the mirror. I see a guy who's really good at what he does who worries too much about my competition. While I'm in it to win it in speaking and podcasting, I've intentionally focused more on me and less on them. I've come to realize that if I'm as good as I think I am, I'll rise to the top. If not, I won't. I was quoted in an interview once saying, "Life is not fair. Fighting is not fair. Good people do not always win. But NEVER shy away from doing what's right. Maintain your integrity through it all." I know my truth, and I'm sticking to it.

About losing listeners

I know that listeners come and go, and I'm okay with that. It's a cost of doing business. Even die-hard listeners who became friends have drifted away. As I saw reflected in Scott Adams's *How to Fail at Almost Everything and Still Win Big*, I have the memories and experiences that those relationships provided at the time, so in my eyes, and I hope the view of the other people, it's a win-win. I'm the same way when listening to podcasts. I have my one or two always-subscribed-to shows, but otherwise I slide from show to show on a regular basis. It's an ebb and flow, and sometimes *The Spaniard Show* is on the outs for some listeners.

I don't know how to think about having lots of listeners. There are ways to increase numbers on podcasts and other social media platforms without really gaining true followers. Strategies exist that get pretty technical, and some are even as blatant as purchasing followers. The underlying reason is that the more listeners you have, the more likely advertisers are willing to pay you to promote on your show and the more money they are willing to give for those promotions. It's certainly important because if the goal is to build a business, money is important, and ads are a source of money. Bigger numbers also serve as marketing for your own products and services. If a million people hear your show a week, versus a thousand, you're likely to get more speaking gigs, sell more shirts, books, online courses, whatever.

I feel compelled to share an important story in my development relating directly to this idea—the amount of downloads I get on my show per month. Some people guard their download numbers, but I've been pretty open about them, mainly because I don't care (it is what it is), but also because my show, in part, is an examination of building a business. If you're into that aspect of the show, it makes sense that I'd share the details.

For the first two years, my numbers were growing relatively consistently. The growth always fluctuated a bit, due to my system of distributing episodes (posting on social media) and depending on the effect from guests re-posting the link as well. For example, Marc Mero, my WWE friend and an uber-active speaker, has half a million loyal fans on Facebook, and he shared the link twice. He goes out of his way to help me grow. That week / month, we had a boom in downloads. But then in October of 2018, there was more than a general fluctuation. During the month of September 2018, we had gotten an all-time high of 21,558 downloads, but then something happened. Something changed in the way downloads are measured / quantified. October saw 17,720, November had 9,756, December had 7,120, and as I sit here typing in my remote office in Panera on January 21, 2019, we're sitting at 7,203 for the month. I have no idea what happened or changed, but this made my heart sink. "We're going down!" I thought. Ugh.

But what I realized was that we were now sitting at the truth. Whether Facebook or social media changed what they counted as a download, or something changed with my podcast host, I now had an accurate number, or at least I had to trust that I did. Maybe my numbers were being inflated by the previous system. I had to come to that realization. But I was certain that the number of people really following my show, my "1000 true fans" as Kevin Kelly says, didn't just drop in half. If they were true fans, they'd find a way to listen. Maybe some of the fair-weather listeners went by the wayside, but the true listeners were still there. My number of downloads might have been cut in half, but my true impact and influence were still the same. A positive side effect of this is that it relieved some of the pressure of posting every episode to every social media platform I have. Now I could focus on really growing The Spaniard's awareness by focusing on the right things and creating better content. Both of these would, in the long run, result in a higher number of downloads.

I'm confident that in the future my podcast will be much like it is today. I absolutely love doing it the way I do it, which allows me to tirelessly put all of myself into it. I do hesitate to speak absolutely when referring to it, though, especially AMXbooks, which I do every day, but from time to time, I do.

I've said more than a few times that I won't stop AMX'ing every day until I physically / mentally am no longer able to do it. But if I'm speaking absolutely 100% truthfully, I actually don't know that. I consider that, at one time, I used to put all of myself into fighting. I'd drive five or more hours in NY / NJ traffic to train for an hour, and back then there was nothing else I'd rather have been doing. But life changes and so do values and preferences. What I do know is that today, there is nothing else in the world I'd rather be doing.

However, as we continue to grow and expand, I do know that some things will change:

Audio quality
I'll have more money to spend on higher-level recording equipment.

Visuals
I'll create a real studio (not a basement "studio"), and I'll add video to record more interviews in person. I'll also have more money to travel and fly in guests.

Advertising
I'll most likely include some advertising in order to monetize the show, though I'm very picky and will wait for the appropriate time and sponsor.

Relatively recently, we established the four channels that I mentioned earlier:

AMXbooks
AMXkids
AMXtalks
AMXweekly

And they feel really right—as have one million previous ideas, so let's let this one play out a bit. Before I say more about that, let me describe how we got there. It took a lot of evolution and willingness to change.

I was open to change

Here's something that Dread said in a discussion on a Dreadisode (AMXtalks 113):

> *Sometimes it's the most important thing to stick to your original plan, and sometimes it's not. It's working on it that's going to teach me the right place for it to go.*

Often, change is best. I'm used to transitions even though they can be difficult. Just ask my wife. Amanda has been the co-pilot to my transitions for the past 14 years. "Your transitions are the most difficult time to be your wife," she says. As a dreamer and a doer, it's very difficult for me to sit and just "be," something I've had to work on, and I feel is an area in which I've improved as of late. Since publishing *DRIVEN* in late 2015, I've been actively learning so much, and we (Dread and I) have done and tried so much that it seems like every day is one transition to another. Nearly every afternoon when I walk upstairs from my office (basement), I am reminded of Vince Lombardi being called "Mr. High-Low" for his emotional swings, as I learned in the book *When Pride Still Mattered*.

It's taken years to get to where I am today in terms of dealing with transitions, and I'm still far away from handling them as efficiently as I'd like. It has taken open and honest communication with Amanda, as well as some knockdown, drag-out arguments that, in retrospect, were the result of my own pent-up stress. Financial freedom is extremely important to me. Not excess, not lavishness, just financial freedom. I want to provide my family with the best of opportunities in life while also helping those around me, and I understand that these transitions, though extremely difficult to endure, are a means to that end. I have a firm belief in the idea of earning things, and though these transitions, at times, seem like the same mazes I see in Gracie's activity books, with most routes having dead ends, I also have a firm belief that I am earning whatever comes, wherever these transitions lead me.

Dread and I often change trajectories. This week, we could be dead-set on getting into more schools. Next week, we could put all of our energy into creating a database full of meeting planners and corporate contacts in an effort to secure more corporate speaking gigs. Within those same weeks, I'll spend a great deal of time worrying about the copy I use on my website homepage. I truly just don't know exactly where I'm going, and the only way to get there is to do: Pick somewhere to go next, and go there. I've attached Speaker, Fighter, Mentor, Author, Media Host, Coach, Consultant and many other titles to my name and business card the past two years in an attempt to explain, to myself as much as anyone, what I do. It's like throwing mud at the wall and seeing what sticks. At times, we've been one inch deep and one mile wide, but I believe our intent is pure and good, and for that, I'm okay with taking a 4-year-old's activity-book-maze approach to achieving my vision ... but it does suck at times.

Changes on the podcast include:

The name of my system
"Addicted to Excellence" became "The Elements of Excellence," which became "AMX."

The name of the podcast
A Fighter's Mindset became *Spaniard101* (at episode #101, no less) which became *The Spaniard Show* (at #188).

The name of my morning show
As mentioned earlier, "Daily Reading" daily (duh) became "AM Excellence" on weekdays, soon shortened to "AMX."

The name of my weekly summary document / episode
As I write this, it's coming up on two years since I created a weekly document to highlight the week's learnings. That helps me catalog what I learn while also offering listeners a tool to use as they see fit. These were the name changes:

3/24/17	Excellence Blueprint
10/13/17	BOLD Blueprint
1/19/18	What I Learned this Week (WIL)
11/16/18	AMXweekly

The way I title morning shows
When I studied Jack Canfield's *The Success Principles* in depth on AMXbooks 422-443, I began to title the episodes after the current book; *i.e.,* "AMXbooks 422 - The Success Principles 1" ... "AMXbooks 423 - The Success Principles 2." That became a permanent pattern. As I write this, today's title is: "AMXbooks 689 - A Walk in the Woods 9."

The overall, umbrella name for the shows

The AMX family, my new learning system, developed: AMXbooks, AMXkids, AMXtalks and AMXweekly

Our practice of splitting episodes

We no longer split episodes as we did in these cases:

AMXtalks #21 and 22:	*DRIVEN*
AMXtalks #35 and 36:	Ben Brenneman
AMXtalks #46 and 47:	Fight Story: Dread about Janet's diagnosis
AMXtalks #49 and 50:	Stitch Duran

Doing episodes ABOUT episodes

We also used to do episodes that were about other episodes (our own episodes or from elsewhere):

AMXtalks #25 about AMXtalks #24, the Frankie Edgar interview
AMXtalks #34 about Rob Dyrdek on *School of Greatness*

I did keep doing this occasionally:

AMXtalks #162 about Ice Cube on *The Big Interview with Dan Rather*
AMXtalks #163 on Jaguars vs. Caimans, from a Nat Geo show

We even had episodes about split episodes!

AMXtalks #53 was about AMXtalks 46 and 47
AMXtalks #51 was about AMXtalks 49 and 50

Doing interviews after all

At first I intended not to conduct interviews, but finally it just made sense. I had set out to not do interviews for the sole purpose of being different. Everyone else was doing interviews, so I wouldn't do interviews! Boo, bad call. I really like interviewing people, and I took to it. I mean really took to it, and a lot of people have told me I'm very good at it. And I had opportunities. I knew interesting people and had connections to more interesting people. An unintended ace up my sleeve, I soon found and believe, is my verified check on Twitter—more people respond to me because I'm verified as being who my account says I am. These conversations became another way for me to learn and share something valuable with my listeners. It made sense for my enjoyment and my core purpose, and it fit the lifelong learning theme of the show that was already developing. It also made sense because there was only so much that Dread and I could discuss before it started to be repetitive. I explained the change on AMXtalks 73, "A New View on Interviews."

Sometimes the interviews come in bunches, such as at the Spartan World Championships in Lake Tahoe, CA, I mentioned earlier. For "work," I get to fly out to Tahoe, record a slew of fascinating interviews in person and then run the race the next day. How stinkin' cool is that?! On top of killer content for the show I'm able to form relationships with awesome people, push myself to the max running the 15-ish mile Beast obstacle race and come home with some lifelong memories. I even brought my buddy Matt with me to be my "tech guy," though our tech was quite minimal. It was an opportunity to have fun with a close buddy and gather some amazing content in the process.

When starting something new, the urge to delay and put

off is strong. There are so many things to consider and get right, and that hinders any action at all. At the beginning, we simply had to start the podcast and believe that "it'll buff out." Here are a few other things that changed as we went along:

Intro music

We used no intro music until Episode 100. Initially, we got right to the punch. Coincidentally or not, Matt, whom I just wrote about, was adamant about his preference for me not having long intros. Quick note: My intro music was written by Dread's son, Ethan, who is the reason we met. He was my Spanish student back when that was my day job.

Intros and outros

I initially recorded the intro and outro for each interview with the guest on the line. What an amateur! The guests don't need / want to hear what I'm intro'ing and outro'ing.

Live events

Our first Spaniard Show LIVE event was episode #30, which we held at the Hollidaysburg Area Public Library in my hometown, whose director happens to be Dread's wife, Janet. Enough people showed up that it was a success. NOTE: At almost every home event I host, I'm good for five or more family members, so no-shows are only *almost*-no-shows.

Nuances of my delivery

A technical aspect of the show that we've refined, and will continue to do so, is my delivery. I've gotten better at connecting points and segueing between them, something that is especially frequent on AMXbooks. I generally cover about three points a day, and they're not all related. I've gotten better at drawing connections and / or transitioning more smoothly. My earlier phrase "The next thing I want to talk about is ..." is now usually just "Moving on..."

Exit lines

My standard send-off at the end of the show evolved from "Be bold" to "See ya!" to "Read a book. Take a pic. Tag me. @charliespaniard," and it's still evolving to this day.

Lighting

I upped the ante during Facebook Live recordings by adding lighting—a pair of desk lamps sent by a listener. (Thanks, Ryan!) My "office" is still quite simple. I believe there's a fitting level of production that, once you reach it, that's all you need, at least early on when resources are scarce. Putting in time and energy to go beyond that threshold won't necessarily reap the same in rewards on the other side. When we're working with a real budget, we'll invest.

Completing the set of content

At the suggestion of my fellow podcaster Jim Harshaw, I began uploading the audio from AMXbooks videos (Facebook Live sessions) to my podcast feed starting in November 2016, I started uploading AMXweekly in May 2017 and started uploading AMXkids to the feed in June 2018.

Here's how a typical week goes

My life is built around learning. I still have to do less-than-stimulating tasks such as uploading files, creating AMX show info and titles, printing, and organizing content, but my daily purpose is to learn and teach. Most weeks, I'll take Saturday or Sunday off, rarely both, but if at all possible, I'll use those weekend mornings to read and think, waking up early and taking advantage of that quiet time. The only real variation in this is that I freakin' LOVE to watch good shows and movies, especially documentaries, and Netflix and Amazon Prime are full of them. If I stay up till 1 AM on a Friday or Saturday, I can usually bank on the extra adrenaline of "It's Saturday / Sunday! Woo!" to get me through the next day. Especially in the last few months, I've experimented with sleep and food such that I eventually arrive at the perfect mix of rest and nutrition. It does me no good to get up butt-crack-of-dawn early if I'm too tired to play with my kids later in the day. I'm still letting go of the bravado I feel from "sacrificing like no one else" for the overall well-being of my life. I still sacrifice like *almost* no one else, but not as much as former Spanny did. Maybe when my kids are older and more self-sufficient.

The Rock calls his AM training session his anchor, and I like the terminology. Reading and training are my anchors. Books are the primary source of my learning, and training is the thing I've always done—it's kept me on track. Both practices have a direct effect on my sense of well-being and completeness. If I'm feeling bad about myself / life, the cure is to read and / or train. I've alternated between reading and training right out of bed. Morning duty with the kids is mine, so timing is always a factor.

Note-taking and highlighting go hand-in-hand with my reading. I'm a very obsessive person, and I'm obsessive about learning. It's gotten such that I've had to remind myself that I read to read, not to take notes, but I also read with the primary intent of teaching what I learn. I was talking to Marc Mero the other day on the phone and referring to my AMXweekly episodes, he said, "Man, you can talk forever. How do you always have something to talk about?!" My response was that I'm always reading, and so I always have something new to talk about. It works toward my greater purpose: If I always have a new / fresh / interesting book / piece of content in my brain, then, hypothetically, I'll always have something of substance on which to speak, on stage or in front of the camera / mic. If I blank, with a quick reflection of "Hmm, what did I read this morning?" I can segue into something that's better than silence.

I like the idea of recording daily, as opposed to batch recording, knocking out a bunch of episodes on one day and then scheduling the posts to be released on certain dates. I see the discipline of daily recording as a way to keep me on the path. I would never think of training really hard several times a day on Monday and then sitting idle for the next six days. Reading and learning is a part of me; I believe that recording daily helps elevate my skills as a speaker / host. It's daily progression. There have been instances that I've either had to pre-record (for instance, when traveling) or have chosen to pre-record (during a family vacation), but I do plan, at this point, for as long as I can, to record daily as often as possible.

Show notes

Show notes have been a huge bonus to the show's production. They're gold. But we haven't quite yet figured out what to do with them. Dread has diligently listened to and noted every AMXtalks to date, often writing narratives several pages long, with quotes and headers to help me prep my AMXweekly docs / episodes, as well as provide a catalog of incredible conversations with incredible people. The notes are book-worthy and may one day be put together as a book.

We found our way through growing pains

It's a pretty smooth operation now. Dread and I have become a cohesive unit. He's able to speak and write in my voice and knows me as well as anyone (Wait a minute, is he writing this now?!) We have passed through the initial growing pains that accompany every person who sets out to do / create something special, and we're learning that the growing pains never go away.

13

What Guides Me

PERSEVERANCE

This chapter has more quotes than others because perseverance comes up a lot in my podcast recordings. As I write this, 2019 has gotten off to a great start with speaking gigs, and perseverance has started to level itself with lifelong learning as one of my top themes. It is prominent in almost every book I read, and I've learned that nothing truly valuable comes without perseverance. It's easy for me to relate to perseverance regarding speaking / podcasting because I have not yet achieved what I want to, despite the work and time invested. Perseverance will always matter to me because I will always reach for what I don't yet have.

In *American Wife*, Taya Kyle says the key to her happiness is "appreciating what I have and what I've done, and realizing that I'll always have something else to do." I resonate with that. I *am* that. I love and appreciate rest and relaxation as much as the next person, but only so much of it. I need to earn my rest. The Rock recently tweeted, "Blood, sweat and respect. First two you give, last one you earn." I want to earn that thing. I want to work for it.

Rule #7 - Pursue what is Meaningful (Not what is Expedient)
The successful among us delay gratification. The successful among us bargain with the future.
Jordan Peterson
12 Rules for Life
AMXbooks 461

Spartan boys were taught two life lessons: 1. Never retreat, and 2. Never surrender.
Dean Karnazes
The Road to Sparta
AMXbooks 284

Despite his lack of natural ability, Steve Martin had "the one element necessary to all early creativity: naïveté."
Steve Martin
Born Standing Up
AMXbooks 475

It was easy to be great ... What was hard was to be good, night after night, no matter what the abominable circumstances.
Steve Martin
Born Standing Up
AMXbooks 478

(This was my commenting on the book) Steve Martin practiced his first act (6 minutes of magic) 4 times / day (5 on Sunday) for 3 years. Over 27,000 minutes!
Steve Martin
Born Standing Up
AMXbooks 476

*(When he started to receive praise) They weren't say-
ing it because I was a great comedian, or even a good
one. They were saying it because I was persistent, and
that persistence was starting to show up in small im-
provements. Potential is all about your willingness to
listen, learn and improve.*
Kevin Hart
I Can't Make this Up
AMXbooks 560

Competing in wrestling and fighting taught me that I
was really good at wrestling and fighting but that I wasn't the
best of the best. But it also taught me that I'm dang near the
best of the best at not stopping and at doing things that other
people aren't willing to do. Odd little experiences taught me
that. For instance, doing a 30-minute treadmill run at 1 AM
after a college wrestling match—after we had showered, eat-
en and gone to bed, and, if I remember correctly, it was prior
to a school break. I was the only one in the gym, if you can
believe that. Or traveling six hours round-trip to train for an
hour, repeated consistently for years, or recording a podcast
episode for 734 straight weekdays, which includes prep and
execution of 30-90 minutes daily. Most people just aren't willing to do those things ... are you? That's what will set you
apart. Perseverance doesn't cost a penny. It's FREE. You can
start not-stopping NOW.

One book that highlights perseverance is Ted Turner's
Call Me Ted. If I wouldn't have read it, I wouldn't have believed the amount of adversity he endured to get where he is.
America's Cup Champion, media impresario, philanthropist,
professional sports team owner—those are just a few of his
titles. But beside those successes is a long line of setbacks and
failures, including having his fortune dwindle from $10 bil-

lion to $2 billion over the course of a few years (Turner's words, "To put this in perspective, I lost nearly $8 billion in roughly thirty months. This means that, on average, my net worth dropped by about $67 million per week, or nearly $10 million per day, every day, for two and a half years."). He also made claims that he / his sports teams just didn't back up. He bought the Atlanta Braves in 1976 and promised a World Series title within five years. They eventually won in 1995. He owned the Atlanta Hawks for 27 years and never won a championship. Even if he had billions to lose, it's relative to the same money pressure that you and I feel. It's hard to stay calm when you NEED something to work and little is working. It doesn't matter if we're talking a thousand dollars, a million or a billion. You keep watching for how long you can keep going and keep wanting to put off folding / giving in until things turn around. I like to use the expression "your championship of the world." For some of my friends, this was literal. They are / were the champions of the world. They held the actual belt. Your own "world championship" could be getting a promotion, passing a test or simply getting out of bed one more day. It's all relative. And the question is the same for everyone: Can you hang in there and keeping doing what is necessary to win your championship?

I can't over-stress how stinkin' hard and frustrating it can be to pursue something truly worthy. It's setback and failure after setback and failure. Then every once in a while, something goes right. Most people can't stomach that amount of failure and frustration, and they fold prematurely. Or they don't grasp that you can fail all the way up to the point of success, or "three feet from gold" (you can read about that in Napoleon Hill's *Think and Grow Rich*) and cash in their chips too early. Your biggest mistake can be quitting and losing the work you put in. I'd much rather have tried and failed than to never have tried. Giving all of my self to / in my pursuits has never led me astray. I'm writing to you today with peace in my soul knowing that I do "my best to become the best that I am capable of becoming" (part of John Wooden's definition of success).

The unsuccessful get halfway to the finish line, then turn around. The successful get halfway, then keep going. Both run the same distance, but only one makes it to the finish line.
Kevin Hart
I Can't Make This Up
AMXbooks 562

(On touring for seven straight years to get his career back under control) It was time for me to take my career back into my own hands and get on my grind again. Within a month, I was on the road, and that's when the quiet storm of Kevin Hart began.
Kevin Hart
I Can't Make This Up
AMXbooks 564

Sometimes you have to say yes to the things you want to say no to so you can raise yourself to a place where you get to say no to more things.
Kevin Hart
I Can't Make This Up
AMXbooks 567

I was an overnight success that was only 16 years in the making.
Kevin Hart
I Can't Make This Up
AMXbooks 569

When I was young, my brother gifted me an inspirational framed poster to hang on my bedroom wall. The words were simple, and as well as I can remember, it was the first time I had ever seen / heard them: "Success is a journey, not a destination." What that means to an aspiring 14-year-old who had at that time experienced a limited amount of winning and losing, and what that means to a 38-year-old who's spent decades winning and losing, and what that means to YOU, sitting there, reading, thinking back on your lifetime of tough stretches, is quite different.

Persevere and look like a genius

One upside of persevering is creative breakthroughs. Here are innovations that developed only because I kept going, and sometimes because I was desperate and simply had to come up with something, anything, for the podcast:

Solosodes
Solosodes are basically monologues in which I tell a story or cover a concept. Perhaps the idea for solosodes occurred because I locked myself out of my house one afternoon and was bored. I decided to lie down on my patio out back and start a Facebook Live. I had no plan and no idea if anyone would pop in. They did, and it turned out to be one of my biggest Facebook Live videos to that point. Looking back, I think it's very likely that particular livestream was a precedent for recording solosodes. Following that sunny afternoon, my confidence in my ability to speak off the cuff was at an all-time high.

Giving out my personal phone number

A daily constant is: I am looking to grow my audience, and I need to build relationships with my followers. So a while back, I figured, what the heck, I'll give out my phone number and invite people to call and talk—ask a question, and let's see if I can help in any way. I gave it out pretty regularly and got a fair amount of calls, but not nearly as many as I expected. To me, this was kind of a mini-phenomenon. I think people were so confused that I'd give out my number that they didn't take me up on it. I was often met with, "Dude, it's really you." I've formed relationships with people who took me up on it. It made sense: Only those who were really into what I was doing would call. The process pre-selected people with whom I had similar interests. NOTE: I did have some foresight. I gave out my Google Voice number, which is connected to my cell phone. I figure if it ever does become a problem, I can just disconnect it from my phone. Safeguard.

Episodes from Skype talks

These are cool. I need content for my show, and I had started doing Skype talks with various groups, mostly individual classrooms. Most of these were unpaid, so in order to recoup some value from it, I'd upload the audio to my podcast feed (with permission from the school).

Episodes from Zoom talks

Same idea as Skype talks. One cool experience from this was working with a company where I would host weekly sessions "doing my thing" as company owner Mitch, my former wrestling coach, had requested. Essentially, that meant: Read books, talk about them and infuse energy into people. This particular series was paid, so it was extra valuable (See

AMXtalks 180, "Telling Another Business About Developing My Business").

Audio from video produced to record audio
Dread reminded me of this one, and I was confused by it even though I did it. Dread, a little help?

This is Dread jumping in. This refers to AMXtalks 122. At the time, we were working with The Spaniard's pal Matt Anderson to create an online video to promote Spanny as a speaker, and we needed some additional voiceover audio clips with high energy. We decided that the best plan was for The Spaniard to go on Facebook Live and record a solosode about the video project and be completely open about recording the audio we needed. So he was simultaneously (a) recording a video on Facebook Live (b) recording a podcast episode and (c) recording audio for a video that is now posted on his web site. It was a behind-the-scenes media production extravaganza, and I have to agree with Spanny: It confuses me even as I explain it. But he did it. Dread out!

Live-recording on the road
At Red Rocks
The first time I live-recorded away from home was on a bachelor party weekend in Denver, and I went to Red Rocks Amphitheatre to run sprints. I hosted a "What I Learned this Week" (which later became AMXweekly).

In an airport
I'm in transit. AMXweekly needs to be recorded. I record. Excess noise ... yep. Oh well.

Outside

These are fun ones. I think specifically of recording at Shank Park near Hershey, PA. Early mornings and afternoons. Mosquitos got me. Rain got me. I even had some deer pass by.

And then comes this. If you only listen to one of my episodes, consider this one ... or maybe don't. I think it's unlike any other podcast episode ever (maybe for good reason).

LIVE AUDIO from Training on Pain Street

This was the description that we published for that unique and bizarre episode, AMXtalks 188:

Here's a short advisory before you listen to this audio of The Spaniard putting himself through a typical hellish workout. PLEASE NOTE: This is an extremely unique piece of audio. The only hallucinogens involved were endorphins, dopamine and serotonin released by a ridiculous degree of getting after it. Be prepared to hear ad libbing, bellowing, blowing, chanting, cheering for one's self, delirious recitations, digital beeps, fake swearing and kid-friendly-crudity, gasping, grappling with demons, grunting, hysterical laughing, karaoke-so-bad-it's-good, invention of lyrics, quoting and misquoting of movies, philosophical ramblings, pleading, rejection of online heckling, speaking in tongues (wait, that part is just Spanish), taunting of imagined adversaries, wheezing and YELLING THAT MAKES THE ROOM VIBRATE. Okay, now you're on your own. This is how winnin' sounds!

If that doesn't make you want to go listen, nothing will.

It's gonna be short, it's gonna be sweet, and it's gonna suuuuuuck.
AMXtalks 188

How 'bout them titles?

Here are some of my better titles from back when I gave each AMXbooks a unique title. I'd record the episode, do the uploading, then think, "Hmph, what was that about? What title could I develop from it?" Truthfully, I was amazed that I was always able to come up with something basically on the spot. I did that for 421 episodes prior to revamping titles to align with the name of the current book I'm covering.

(These were all episodes of AMXbooks)

8	Do You Have the I Disease?
15	You Might Be Wrong
16	Shut Up and Listen!
19	Wanna Know the Magic Phrase?
28	So You're Sayin' There's a Chance?!
46	Pressure Schmessure
53	Truth or ... Truth
129	The Word That Can Change It All
140	How to Run a Mile
228	"They"
254	Zero to Zero
269	A Man of Many
277	What's Your Point?
292	It's Just a Cookie
316	Cause Spaniard Said So!
319	Swagger
323	Al Bundy
325	It's Been Good, Boom
329	Just Like Summer Camp

334	Lil Bit of Crazy
342	Yoda
369	Put on Your Boots
370	Critics are Like Farts
373	Let's Talk Ice Cream
378	500 Cases of Chocolate
403	Call Me, Maybe?
405	Fe*
408	I Am
410	Go Flow, Yo!

*An ode to my friend / UFC fighter Frankie Edgar, or Fe (iron)

There isn't a race I've been in where you don't go: 'I just want to quit.' It's the same in business some days: 'I just don't know if I can do this again.' But you do it, and that's how you get ahead. Because the other guy does quit. The other guy isn't willing to do it.
Drew Swope
Entrepreneur and fellow Hollidaysburger
AMXtalks 114

Karnazes states that the first marathon was completed with an incredible gift we all share, the ability to put one foot in front of the other.
Dean Karnazes
The Road to Sparta
AMXbooks 279

Success is not a matter of mastering subtle, sophisticated theory, but rather of embracing common sense with uncommon levels of discipline and persistence.
Patrick Lencioni
5 Dysfunctions of a Team
AMXbooks 413

Shrugging off flaws, failures and mishaps

To say that Dread and I are bootstrapping overstates what we're actually doing—that doesn't do justice to boots and straps. They are too high-class for us. Every morning for AMXbooks, I literally walk down to my basement (freezing cold in winter / hot as ba!!s in summer) and try not to (1) knock things off my desk (2) tip over my cheap tripod before I get my iPhone straight and (3) hit LIVE before my unfinished ceiling, filthy concrete floor and dirty laundry are out of view. It won't always be this way, but currently it is. (I'd like to add in here, several months after writing the above, I've graduated to recording out of my 2010 Subaru Legacy. It's my "mobile office" that I gave the address 2010 Legacy Lane. We recently sold our house and are in a temporary apartment. Who knows, by the time I write my third book, I could be recording on out of a bus shelter … or on your street corner.)

Another barrier to flawless episodes is less-than-optimal internet connections and / or bad links (the thing that's supposed to connect us doesn't work). My worst experience with this was with Amelia Boone, Obstacle Course Racing (OCR) world champion and corporate attorney. Not attorney before becoming OCR world champion—she does them simultaneously. SHE DOES NOT HAVE TIME TO WASTE. I had to call her back three different times because our internet connection and / or software was breaking down. We'd get a few minutes into it then I'd have to interrupt and say, "I'm so sorry, Amelia. My recorder didn't record. Can we start over? … "I'm sorry my internet cut us off. Can we try again?" Nothing like having a conversation for the first time for the third time. Thank goodness she's such a kind person, because she was as patient and understanding as I could have asked for.

Other flubs include:

Editing mistakes pointed out by listeners

One episode had lots of silence at the end—like an hour of it. Dread tells me that was caused by his accidentally messing up the loop region, whatever that means. C'mon, man! There was also one episode where the audio came out of only one speaker / earphone—no stereo sound. That time, Dread's excuse was unbalanced pan. Again, I have no clue what that means, but ... seriously, Dread, get on the stick.

Misnumbering that created two of AMXbooks 86

Don't tell anyone, but the numbering of every episode since AMXbooks 86 has been off by one. I didn't realize it until way after the fact. Let's keep it our little secret.

Bad luck with an over-the-web recording service

It sounded easier than what we were doing, but because of different computer recording speeds, it caused lots of extra editing work for Dread.

Mindset & Toughness Camp

This was one of my million-dollar ideas to bring together hundreds of young student-athletes who were focused on developing their mental and physical abilities. I pushed it for months on the podcast and appearances, and I think we had one sign-up.

AMX Fight Club

AMXFC for short. This was cool. A good start. At one point, I had about 20 members paying $10/month. The odd part about AMXFC is that I never truly knew what it was. It was almost as if people believed in this thing that I was building so much that they were paying for the energy that they got from the show. I did produce extra content and send out AMXFC-member-only emails, but eventually I closed up shop. I just couldn't put my finger on what exactly it was.

AMX-tended

AMX-tended (AMXT) was yet another million-dollar idea that didn't endure. AMXT was my belief that there were —and my attempt to bring together—hundreds of people who loved reading and talking about books so much that they would pay $100 / month for weekly virtual hangouts / masterminds / book talks. It actually had some legs, but the legs grew tired in time. I write more about AMXT in the next chapter, about belief.

Failed predictions

In AMXtalks 151, ("Farewell 2017, Hello LIMOUSINE IN 2018"), I predicted BIG things in 2018. The result: Not so many BIG things. Earlier in 2017, Dread foresaw another book by January 2018 (AMXtalks 48). That didn't happen. Hey, at least we're not off by 14 years like Ted Turner was with his Braves predictions. (Not as I write this, anyway.) He lived, so will we.

Speak Spanish with Spaniard

Because I'm teaching my kids Spanish, I figured I'd foray into teaching Spanish via the podcast. It was okay for a bit, but the lack of listener interaction was surprising. I received only a handful of topics on which listeners wanted me to teach. I burned through them pretty quickly. Dead after 11 episodes. ¡Muerto!

Spaniard's Weekly Workouts

I get a lot of questions about training. I decided to do an audio rundown of each week's training on the podcast. It lasted four episodes. Didn't work out (get it???).

Every adversity carries with it the seed of an equivalent benefit.
Napoleon Hill
On the Air!
AMXbooks 220

17.5% of middle-classers agreed with "Failure has taught me what I'm good at," while 94.9% of ultra-high-net-worthers ($30 million +) did.
Dr. Cindra Kamphoff
Beyond Grit
AMXbooks 416

A lot of people are okay with failure, but they like to rename it "a learning experience." I get it, but if we really want to demystify and deconstruct it and take away the scariness of it, then let's just be okay with using the word.
Andrea Waltz
Sales Trainer / Co-Author of Go for No
AMXbooks 155

You're going to understand that failure is the thing that makes you great. It's embracing the struggle. It's being able to understand that failure is nothing but learning. You have to be able to process each separate episode and compartmentalize it and understand what it is.
Jeff Campbell
NFL Veteran
AMXtalks 191

There is victory in defeat. Following Boom Boom's first title fight loss, commentator / former champ Sean O'Grady said, "He's won my heart." The world agreed.
Mark Kriegel
The Good Son
AMXbooks 318

At the time of this writing, I can think of eight major goals I've had in my life: Elementary state title, PIAA state title, straight A's in high school, All-American in college, straight A's in college, straight A's in graduate school, UFC contract, UFC title. Of those eight major life goals, I've accomplished only three of them. Setting goals is not all about accomplishing them—it's about pursuing them. Setting every one of those life goals has played a major role in helping me live the full life that I've lived.

It took many, many years of setting and falling short of goals until I defined "success" for myself and truly appreciated the process of pursuing goals. Fighting in the UFC was a personal and professional goal of mine. I had given every ounce of my being to make it happen. Signing a contract with the UFC was the maximum achievement for a professional MMA fighter. I had done it.

I have done a lot of things in my life, actually, and I still do a lot of things. I win some of them, I lose some of them. And I'm okay with that. When you live life like I do, setting and pursuing extraordinary goals, you are going to fail much more often than the average person.

Looking back on my record of wins and losses (of all kinds, not just fighting), it seems like there was more heartache than happiness. Athlete or not, we all win and lose in life—relationships, promotions, health and fitness, and so on—but is it the wins and losses that define our success?

In today's society, one that offers trophies and awards for everyone on the field, I don't share the same sentiment. There are winners and losers. There are high achievers and low achievers. We are not all the same. I am not offering a "win all" for everyone. I am simply offering my perspective after 25+ years of winning and losing at the highest levels of competition and life.

Finding myself able to get knocked out cold on national television and get back up is a lesson that, at the time, I sure as heck would have chosen NOT to learn. But in hindsight it was one of many instances, albeit the most intense, that taught me the ability to fail and get back up. I literally had no other choice. With the doctor's assistance, I came to, and I had no action to choose other than to stand up and shake my opponent's hand. It just so happened to be in the middle of a cage on a live broadcast for everyone to see. I'm not proclaiming that I did it to highlight the symbolic meaning of getting back up after getting knocked down—I just had no other option. I look back on that instance as one of the most powerful of my life, right up there with losing my second state title in a row during my senior year of high school. Failing sucks, especially in the public eye, but boy does it carry with it an incredibly valuable bonus: You gradually become fearless. What I actually mean is *functionally* fearless.

Having no fear of failing on a public stage has made everything that much easier while building a business. My daily norm while fighting was to travel from Point A to Point B and fight someone. There was a physical price to pay for failing. Nowadays, it's so much easier to fail because no one is actually inflicting damage on me. It's like a party every time I fail and no one punches or kicks me. No one even tries to choke me anymore!

Scott Adams talks about failing forward in his book *How to Fail at Almost Everything and Still Win Big*. Heck, he describes the book as "a semi-entertaining tale about a guy who failed his way to success." The idea in itself is not revolutionary—we've all heard that success is attached to failure—but the way that Adams presents it is unique, and that's why I'm referencing it now. "Failure always brings something valuable with it. I don't let it leave until I extract the value," says Adams. He highlights the skills and people you acquire along the way.

I had never thought of it that way: The people, the skills. Yes, this particular project / idea / event might have fallen flat, but look at the know-how you now possess and the relationships you've developed as a result.

Couple that with famed football coach Bill Walsh's saying about learning from losing and failure—"but what I took from it was …" (which I discovered in his book *The Score Takes Care of Itself*)—and the moral of the story becomes quite clear: Wring the neck of failure for everything it's worth!

I kept going even though NOBODY CARES

One of the most surprising realities I've learned is the general apathy that exists amongst listeners. It's not that they're mean or vindictive, they just don't care or take action the majority of the time. More accurately, only a very, very, very, very small percentage of people take action. Yes, I have a loyal crew of early adopters, but even amongst the hardest core listeners, the response rate is REALLY low. I think it's the reality of people: They just don't take action often. It's also quite possible that I've been offering the wrong thing to the right people, but either way, the response rate to my calls to action tells me that apathy is there and / or something is off. (A call to action is a request or proposal that gets your audience to do something: Sign up for this and get this thing, order now and get a percentage off, and so on).

Here are some specific examples of failed calls to action:

Requests for contact

In every outro from every show—so that means at least seven times a week—I make specific requests: Leave a review on iTunes, email me, text me, call me. These appeals are almost never answered.

Offers of show notes

During the period when Dread would literally put hours into creating Show Notes, I offered them to listeners who joined my email list. It didn't entice them to sign up.

Offers of my weekly notes

For over a year, I offered a weekly email with a link to download my notes from the week's episodes. Originally, as I mentioned earlier, this was the Excellence Blueprint, later the Bold Blueprint, then What I Learned This Week, and now AMXweekly—except by the time we got to "AMXweekly," I had stopped sending the email. Basically, no one ever downloaded the document.

Merch

Dread spent yet more hours designing a cool logo for AMX, and it was exciting to announce that it was available on T-shirts. But the day after I gave the news in the episode and wore the shirt online while recording AMXbooks, I gave this summary on the next episode:

We sold ONE shirt yesterday in the giant AMX T-shirt launch. One shirt! That was, like, 20 bucks, and I spent 60 in shipping free ones out to people, so we are on a business ROLL!
AMXtalks 122

It's a grind to build listenership

Outstanding stories and guests (and my show has them every week) are not enough. That's the reality. You've got to do more to make it happen.

When Dread and I started the podcast, I set an initial goal, a marker, of 1 million downloads, meaning that my show has been listened to 1 million times. It served, and still does, as my guiding light (part of Element #1, Vision). Downloads are one of the easiest metrics to track in podcasting "success," so that was my line of thinking: Assess the show based on number of downloads. At the time of this writing, to the minute on April 2, 2019, I have 428,506 downloads. With a thirst for success and a bottomless well of Spaniard to share, my impulse yearns for fast growth. I want more NOW. I have to remind myself, quite often, that we're playing the long game. Thinking back, my road to the UFC was a three-year process AFTER a lifetime of wrestling. Fortune was in my favor, and at the end of the day, luck played a big part.

A podcaster friend of mine, Anthony, put it to me in a way that helped keep things in perspective. Paraphrased, he said, "Don't measure your success in downloads. That's only one metric." This plays into the idea that there are many ways to measure success, and by combining them into a system that makes sense to you, you can't lose. Add to the number of downloads other aims such as these: Impact, new relationships, new project ideas and skills developed in the process.

These are just a few of the additional metrics of success that apply to something as simple as podcasting.

I kept going despite rejection

(On his early days in Hollywood) "No" became as much a part of my life in LA as traffic jams and parking tickets.
Kevin Hart
I Can't Make this Up
AMXbooks 563

A short lesson on perspective: Picture a circle. Now put a dot in the center. That dot is you, and that circle encompasses your hopes, dreams, goals and visions. Inside that circle is a select few people whose mission is to help you achieve your dreams. EVERYONE else is outside that circle. That doesn't make them good or bad, nice or mean, supportive or non-supportive. It just makes them outside of your circle. They have their own circles with their own hopes, dreams, goals and visions. They have their own select few. Every once in a while your circle will overlap with theirs, and you will be in each other's circles, but most times that will only be temporary. Sometimes, your circles will not overlap, and you will no longer be in each other's circles. Your hopes, dreams, goals and visions will not overlap, and you will not be each other's primary focus points. It can sound a bit cheap and transactional, but it's not. It's simply the way it is. "What can you do for me now?" is a way to look at it, except for those in your circle at all times. Think of it this way: Your health is very important to me, but the health of my wife and kids is more important to me than your health. That doesn't make me a jerk, it's just the way it is. People have their priorities, and sometimes you will be part of their priorities and sometimes, you won't. Your Circle of Helpers will change with time. Don't take it personally. That's taken me a lot of practice.

> *We're doing what we're learning. That's how it's done. That's Spaniard 101. It's not learning and then sitting and not doing, it's learning and then doing. So win, lose, draw, good, bad, ugly, it doesn't matter, because we're doing it. So in five years, ten years, twenty years —maybe on my grave?—we can look back and say, "Yeah, man, this is it."*
> **AMXtalks 124**

> *The reason that in twenty years, "The Spaniard" and my show will be big is because I just won't stop until it is, period.*
> **AMXtalks 173**

> *Every once in a while, I'll be sitting in my office and / or my basement, busting my butt, thinking, 'Is this really reaching people?' And then I'll get an email or a comment from someone, and it totally reinvigorates or re-emphasizes the good in what we're creating.*
> **AMXtalks 65**

I have struggled through the difficulty of continuing

On one of the many days I've felt like throwing in the towel, Dread said to me, "Do you have anything better to do?" That means that even if things aren't going well, you're in the right place if it's your highest calling. Do you have something else more valuable to do? No? Then keep doing what you're doing. Once you act on that, it simply becomes a matter of bearing the difficulty and frustration of "it" not working.

When I slip, Dread helps me course-correct. For the longest time, I was getting up at 4:30 AM like clockwork. Boom! I'm up ready to roll. Then summer 2018 hit, and I laid off the gas pedal a bit. A bit turned into laying off the gas pedal a lot, and hitting snooze became a regular occurrence. I went from waking up at 4:30 to snoozing until after 6. "It's summer," I told myself. This carried into the fall, and I didn't like it. Dread shook me straight. I set up a phone call and laid it out on the table, going all the way back to the summer and my reasoning for why it was so. He hashed it over and sent back a response that changed my trajectory, "I think you just need to man up and do it." I manned up on the spot and started NOT hitting snooze. I found my wake-up time. Attitude is everything, and sometimes the right words from the right person will do the trick. Just stay on the rocky path toward success. It's most always rocky.

As previously mentioned, John Wooden's definition of success is one of my favorites: "Peace of mind which is a direct result of self-satisfaction in knowing you did your best to become the best you are capable of becoming." Wooden led a value-oriented life and was one of the best coaches of all time. He reinforces that you can do it the right way.

Wooden also says, "Make no mistake: We all want to win the race. Whether in basketball, business, or another competitive arena, victory can be glorious." Who doesn't want to win? Victory can indeed be glorious, but it's certainly not the only thing. It needs to be coupled nicely with an awareness of the process and the intent to do / be your best.

I began to process this deeper meaning of success later in my career. The cycle of professional fighting is much like this: Fight, relax for a time, train hard, wait several months, fight again, repeat. If you win, those several months are filled with a mix of relief, feel-good-ness, belief, reassurance in the life-style you've chosen and the sacrifices you make and overall positivity. If you lose, however—and in professional fighting it's bound to happen—you experience the exact opposite feelings: Pressure, doubt, questions and overall negativity. I found myself on the losing end of a few high-profile fights and fell into the latter scenario: A negative couple of months for every loss that I'd encounter. The gloom began to get, for lack of a better word, annoying. I was not okay with feeling how I felt. I'd wake up in the middle of the night and think, "Yes! Life is good. I'm the best!" OR "Ugh, did I really just get choked out on national television?"

I wanted something more out of my life and experiences, so I started looking around and taking notes. How exactly did the highest performers in the world, the best of the best, come to grips with winning and losing? None of this is easy. There is no fast-tracking or eliminating the heartbreak felt upon falling short of a dream or blanking at the decisive moment. That's all just part of the game.

14
What Guides Me

BELIEF

This chapter is like a separate book in itself because it's both about HAVING belief and RECEIVING belief. It's about maintaining and projecting belief even when:

- What you do is hard to explain, which is often

- It doesn't seem to make sense, which is often

- You keep failing, which is often

- Negative thoughts fill your mind, which (if you're anything like me) is often

I've read a lot about the 1% or 2% of early believers, but what I have found is even harsher than that: A lot of that 1% or 2% come and go, leaving only the truest of "true believers," and they are very, very few. So it's a lot less than 1%.

But that fraction of 1% is hard-core. They believe in you more than you do, as Dread does with me. If I'm confident in myself, Dread is super-duper-times-1-million confident in me.

It's frustrating to envision something so clearly but have difficulty putting it into form for others to so clearly see. Here are some of my current thoughts on that process:

When even your strongest
believers don't take action

It's just that natural flow of human dynamics. None of us responds that often. That puts it on me to give them a reason to respond. This, in the long run, has been helpful.

When even your strongest
believers don't follow through

I've had some really good people reach out and offer help / services, and either because of my poor communication / leadership, or the reality of the grunt work involved, it's still just me and Dread. It's not good or bad, it just is.

When your believers come and go

When I think back, it makes me smile to think of all the great conversations I've had with my biggest believers. Almost immediately, though, that smile turns to a look of confusion: What happened to them? Where did they go? Whatever the reason, the frequency and intensity of communication with 99% of my early adopters is non-existent. Others have come and taken their place, and a very, very few are still around. I suppose in the long run, after this cycle happens 10 or 20 times, we'll have a core group of "early" adopters. Again, the onus is on me, not them.

(Quote from Caryl Stewart, who sub-let the first scoop shop) There was a sense from the beginning that this was something special.
Fred "Chico" Lager
Ben & Jerry's: The Inside Scoop
AMXbooks 375

Here's a crazy fact: We have 50,000 conversations with ourselves every day, and 40,000 of them are negative!
Jack Canfield
The Success Principles
AMXbooks 479

"No future in coaching. Try something else." (Said to Vince Lombardi when he applied for college jobs)
David Maraniss
When Pride Still Mattered
AMXbooks 247

Grandfather presents man as an island, made up of concentric circles, each one a level of potential. The ego/I/self is the most primitive level, a prison in which we are held captive by doubt, fear and limitations.
Tom Brown, Jr.
Awakening Spirits
AMXbooks 37

(Quote from Vince Lombardi) I'll never be a head coach. I'm 42 years old and no one wants me. Nobody will take me.
David Maraniss
When Pride Still Mattered
AMXbooks 253

Lanny Watts, a plumber, was offered free ice cream for life in exchange for his services. He asked, "Well, does this cover your franchises?"
Fred "Chico" Lager
Ben & Jerry's: The Inside Scoop
AMXbooks 374

(On Joe Kenn, master strength coach) Whatever expectation I had of myself, where I thought, "I can't go faster, I can't grow stronger, I can't push past this," he snapped that over and over until I realized: There is no ceiling. He pushed me beyond what I thought I was capable of so many times that I realized: It is whatever's in my mind, and I can go further and be better than what I ever thought.

Kyle Kingsbury
Former UFC Fighter / Host, Kyle Kingsbury Podcast
AMXtalks 189

(On his mentor, Dai Vernon, "The Man Who Fooled Houdini") I didn't know it wasn't possible. He was the top of the world for 60 years, but he pushed me past what he had achieved and worked on himself.

Richard Turner
World's Greatest Card Mechanic
AMXtalks 176

Maybe someone able-bodied sees a six-foot wall. We see a challenge that some of these guys were told: You're never going to accomplish it. Some of them can, and some other ones need help. Now they know that they have someone behind them.

Earl Granville
Combat Amputee / Member of Operation Enduring Warrior
AMXtalks 132

Steve Martin gave himself two rules on stage: (1) Never let them know I was bombing and (2) Make the audience believe I thought I was fantastic, that my confidence could not be shattered.

Steve Martin
Born Standing Up
AMXbooks 477

My history of struggling to believe

Every single morning, I see this backpack, I kind of feel it on my back. It's full of rocks: Doubt, negativity, "Can I do this?" "Is it worth it?" I consciously have to force myself to take it off.
AMXtalks 162

I was on a roll. My career was blossoming. I had just beaten up one of the toughest guys on the planet, and it was smooth sailing for The Spaniard. Little by little, though, the trials of life started to mount. I began to feel the wear and tear of life on the road, and being several hours away from the people I loved was becoming unbearable. I was becoming jaded. I needed a change. I made a change. I moved back to PA (from NJ) and shifted my training to a new "team." I use "team" loosely because, in actuality, there was no continuity between my trainers. While they were all tremendous individuals and trainers, they were in different towns or states. I was the only constant.

My brother / advisor, Ben ("ChAd" for Chief Advisor) took notice and brought it to my attention. I ignored him. "What does he know?" I thought. On the contrary, I knew what I was doing. Right. Well, I know now. I was acting out of disillusionment. The result of knowing what I was doing? A knockout loss on live national television—the most vulnerable state I've ever been in. I had unknowingly allowed my negative attitude to have total control and dictate my actions. I was starting to get sour, and I didn't like it. I still had a lot to learn.

Thankfully, amazing teachers are in reach of any of us. Nowadays, because I no longer have a gym full of hungry animals to keep me in check, I've turned nearly full time to books and conversations to keep my mind operating at a high level, combatting the self-doubt that tries to rear its ugly head. Time devoted to learning is a structured part of my day; it's fuel.

In his book *The Four Agreements*, based on ancient Toltec wisdom, Don Miguel Ruiz identifies four agreements that will lead to a life of happiness and love. "Be impeccable with your word" is one of those agreements, and he's not just referring to the words you use on others, he's also referring to the words you use on yourself. When it comes to myself, I'm not sure I'll ever be impeccable with my word, but I now know the formula for making the deficit null and void: Fill it with hard work and positive "stuff." Silence the negative hum of your mind by placing a giant drum of positive energy right next to it, and pound the living daylights out of it.

Sometimes it's not about being positive or negative, it's about being mindful. Mindfulness is a mental state achieved by focusing one's awareness on the present moment. What? Huh? "Mindfulness is fufu stuff, weird, not for me," said me to me for much of my life. Then I read Phil Jackson's book *Eleven Rings: The Soul of Success*, and all that changed. *Eleven Rings* is a book that highlights Jackson's leadership and life philosophies. This was the guy who coached Michael Jordan, Dennis Rodman and Kobe Bryant, just to name a few, all the while figuring out what makes himself tick and sharing it with those around him. He led the Chicago Bulls to two different three-peats (winning three NBA championships in a row on two separate occasions). Incredible.

I often judge a book as "good" by taking away at least one nugget of insight, wisdom and / or philosophy that I implement into my life moving forward, and one of the pieces I took from Jackson's book was this idea of mindfulness. He presented it in a way that made sense to me: "Remembering to come back to the present moment." That's it. Mindfulness is simply being present and aware. Looking back on all of my losses and setbacks, the vast majority of them were due to not being present. I was off in my mind worrying about other things that had nothing to do with the here and now.

A QUICK ASIDE: Stories of early believers

Here are a few anecdotes I often turn to for encouragement: Lady Gaga grew from her 1%. No one else "got" her music. Scott Adams followed his 2% of people who "got" Dilbert. Seth Rogen believed he was funny due to making his one friend Evan Goldberg laugh. If you can make one person laugh, you've got something, right?

Gratitude for my early supporters

My family has supported me for my entire life, right up through my wrestling and fighting careers. The sacrifice and commitment it took on their part to help me pursue my dreams will never be forgotten. In *DRIVEN* I proudly and humbly tell the lengths they went to. It's something I'll pay forward to my own kids.

And then came my non-family early supporters. One of the neatest experience I've had is seeing them surface. People coming out of the woodwork to offer a hand or express interest in helping and supporting. Whether or not it actually developed into something is almost irrelevant. It was their intention that meant the world to me. These are notes about many of them:

Dave. (Hear him on AMXtalks 42 and 178) Our work together around exercise and weight management has served in so many helpful ways. Though we don't still work together, the lessons and friendship remain.

Ashleigh. (Read more about her in Chapter 16) A hugely important fight fan turned friend. She and Dave essentially own that category. Like me, she battles doubt and negativity, but I have been able to help her in some way, and likewise, her belief in me helps me. The best kind of relationship.

Darlene. She represents one of my most valuable learning experiences—that for one reason or another, listeners come and go. Life interrupts. Her energy and belief sustained me for quite some time, and for that, I'm very thankful.

Coach Friday. (Hear him on AMXtalks 86) He saw something in me, and he pounced. He's the type of guy who puts his money where his mouth is. He believes, and he *does*.

Pritch (AMXT). He probably carries the flag for the early adopters with whom I still talk regularly. Teacher, coach, friend. I even stayed at his house the night before I did an assembly at his school (which he set up). I did a thousand push-ups and livestreamed AMXbooks from his spare room.

Dennis. Another listener turned friend whose belief and participation (as well as sarcastic humor) on my livestreams fuels (and annoys) me daily.

Shak (AMXT). (Hear him on AMXtalks 116) I coached him at East Stroudsburg University as I got my master's. He is a taker of *The Spaniard Show* pill. Shak gets it, and his ceiling is sky-high. We communicate almost daily.

Lee (AMXT). (Hear him on AMXtalks 102) Can you imagine someone appreciating what you do so much that they send you checks every so often to say, "What you're doing is special. You deserve to be rewarded for it"? That's Lee. He even brought my wife and I to NYC and put us up in a RITZ CARLTON. Just the day before I wrote this I got a piece of mail from Lee. He's a special man that represents energy and relentlessness. He goes after it.

Craig (AMXT). Craig from Scotland is the man. One of the handful of early listeners with whom I interact regularly to this day. He just sent me a Facebook message the morning that I wrote this. Business owner, into martial arts, family man. Another cool friendship from the show.

Byron (AMXT). Byron was a grade behind me in high school. We didn't have a personal relationship until he reached out to me post-fighting, but we sure clicked. Early on, he was a part of nearly everything I tried. Stand-up dude.

Ben (AMXT). A lawyer with gnarled BJJ/cauliflower ears who loves books. Could there be a cooler combination? He writes and publishes MMA articles, too.

Chad (AMXT). (Hear him on Episodes 110 and 119) An early adopter who took me up on giving out my number. He called, we clicked. While on business in Philly, he came to my house. We trained and hung out.

Drew. (Hear him on AMXtalks 114) What a standup guy whose desire to see me succeed is pure. We haven't quite figured out (and maybe never will) how to connect what he does and what I do, but his belief in me, and his credibility as a man and businessman helps me move the needle forward.

Dr. Tom. (Hear him on AMXtalks 96) Friend, supporter, businessman. He is extremely successful. He has boosted my income by paying very good rates for one-on-one jiu-jitsu and wrestling sessions for years. My gut sense is that he just wants to see his friend succeed, and it's the least he can do. His least is my most.

Sugar. (We came up with a nickname to protect his identity at his request) A real life Rain Man. And early Spaniard supporter. We don't talk much anymore, but he's still listening. He also helped proof this book.

Nick (*aka* Spice; AMXT). Part of our early-morning-Saturday-work foursome while we had it (along with Dread and Sugar), Nick has been a constant. We've talked a lot over the last few years, and he's always stayed a part of what I'm doing. He, too, spent time at my house.

AMXT

I mentioned earlier that as part of developing the business of The Spaniard, I have experimented with various programs to monetize my content. None of them has been "the one," but they've all taught me something to use moving forward. The most intense program I've had thus far is AMXtended (AMXT). It was an extension of AM Excellence (AMX), hence the name. It was a group of highly-motivated, ambitious guys (gals were welcome as well) who appreciate learning and pushing ourselves physically and mentally. When I began giving out my number on the show, I expected to be bombarded with junk and hate messages; I was thinking with an MMA mindset here, as MMA doesn't have the most considerate fans. Instead, I was met with an exceptionally high number of supportive inquiries that have developed into real, genuine relationships, both business and personal.

There were eight members in AMXT, and every one signed up at the beginning; no one else signed up after the kickoff. Why? I dunno. I very much enjoyed the environment of AMXT. Those eight guys were part of my inner circle. Some still are. It was a neat dynamic. I trusted them, and they trusted me. I held them accountable. I called them on their BS, and we worked to figure it out. I helped them stay on course. We had a very open, honest relationship within the group. It got uncomfortable at times, but that's the only way to get to the top. These guys saw something special in me and my message and were appreciative and excited to be a part of that journey. They were a special group. Out of the thousands of people who've had the opportunity to call or text me, only a handful have, and these guys were among them.

AMXT eventually fizzled, but I look back fondly at this time and reflect on our Friday afternoon group calls as a formative part of my development as a speaker and facilitator.

Other supporters come and go, then there's Dread

As you'll read in this book and can hear on my podcast, my unpaid business partner, Dread, has been a staple in my life the last few years. He gets me, personally and creatively, but he isn't a Yes Man. Much of the wisdom you hear from me comes from him. Often, his words become my words. When someone comes to you and says, "I just want to help. Forget about money. I don't want anything. And hey, if you get famous, I get famous!"—as Dread did, in those exact words —you know they're on board for the right reasons.

Here's how I met him. One of my junior high students was Dread's son Ethan, or "Incendio" in class. Dread has always been the kind of guy who is interested in creative and artistic stuff, things that are full of expression. Initially, I was simply Incendio's Spanish teacher who used to be a good wrestler. That changed, and our trajectory changed, when Dread saw me on *Pros vs. Joes*. He saw me as a guy who was going after something, taking a chance, putting myself out there, and my best guess is that he simply wanted to be around it, to see if there was a chance of creating something together. His initial idea was a comic book telling my story. He's also very attached to our community—his wife Janet runs the public library in my hometown. A few hiccups arose when we sifted through my *Pros vs. Joes* contract (I couldn't tell the story in something like a comic book), so we came up with a few more quirky ideas that make me smile in a sort of "Ummmm" kind of way. If you look hard enough on Youtube you can find a video of me wrestling a giant blow-up dinosaur—that was a Dread production. "I Challenge Charlie" is another one of his ideas that I look back on fondly. It was an event where I took on school kids in a variety of wacky challenges—cup-stacking (which was a thing back then), typing, push-ups, looking up a word in the dictionary, jacks (tabletop, not jumping). Good times. One the next page is the poster that Dread created, with art by his son Incendio:

The Hollidaysburg Area Public Library invites kids and their families and friends to

I CHALLENGE CHARLIE!

Kids versus Charlie Brenneman in fun events!
Thursday, December 7, 7:00 pm at the Library

THE MAN:

Teacher

Wrestling champion

Reality TV champion

Hollidaysburg native

Funny guy!

THE EVENTS:

Math Ages 7-11
Jacks Ages 7-11
Situps Ages 12-15
Typing Ages 7-11
Spelling Ages 7-11
Drawing Ages 7-11
Pushups Ages 12-15
Memorizing Ages 7-11
Hair braiding Ages 7-11
Cup stacking Ages 4-6
Google search Ages 7-11

As our relationship grew, and when I decided to write my first book, Dread reached out, and our current path was set. He had experience self-publishing books, and he possesses a creative and functional skill set that serves us in every way. We worked for dozens of hours on *DRIVEN*, sifting through it with a fine-toothed comb. I sat beside him as he did what I did not know how to do. There's A LOT that goes into self-publishing a book. We learned a lot about each other sitting side by side for 12 hours a day. I learned quickly that he produces (mostly) bad jokes non-stop, and one of his standbys is that his last name, Eldred, comes from the Spanish words "El Dread." Now, "dread" isn't a Spanish word, and Sr. El Dread ain't so scary, but still, I took to it and have called him "Dread" ever since. Yes, he has a first name, but I now have little use for it. As far as I'm concerned, he's Dread.

From the beginning, Dread and I had a shared vision. He saw me as having all of the components for a career helping people get the most from themselves. At the time, we made a lot of comparisons to Tony Robbins (Shoot for the top, right?). He eventually said that he was ready to help me any way that he could, and I took him up on it. He actually said to me, "Look, I don't want any money. I just want to help." Coming from MMA, this was music to my ears. I had gotten a bit jaded from the sport. Dread does anything and everything: Editing, designing, writing, brainstorming, planning. He brings a lot to the table. He went to college on an academic scholarship and graduated first in his class in both high school and college. He has written eight self-published books and has spent years working on his masterpiece novel *Rubrum*. The title is Latin for "Red," and you can see it at www.thisis.red.

There have been some notable developments in his life during our work together. Dread wrote and performed a one-man play to express appreciation for his workplace after he passed his 25-year anniversary there. You can hear about it in episodes AMXtalks 20, "How to Speak for 90 Minutes Without Notes," and AMXtalks 113, "How It Feels To Finally Create What You Wanted." During this time Dread has also been working with his wife Janet to form the best response to her diagnosis of early-stage dementia. For now, that basically means she has a lot of memory problems, but dementia is usually a degenerative disease, so she and Dread have to watch for decline. In the past few years, Janet has also developed epilepsy, having seizures during which she would go vacant. These are now controlled by medicine. Dread helps her keep up with her prescriptions and appointments. He talked about these things in episodes AMXtalks 46 and AMXtalks 47, "Fight Story: Facing Disease with Gratitude." Dread ended up taking early retirement to put more time into helping me and doing his own writing, knowing that he wanted Janet to see him make these efforts before it became too late.

Dread and I have talked for countless hours at all times of the day and night. One of the most memorable times was during a drive home from West Point. I had gone up to West Point (another idea / opportunity), and he knew that I would be driving back late at night. He went to bed early and woke up about midnight, and we talked for a couple hours. I'm forever grateful and look forward to continued growth and experience together. I even wrote him a poem and read it on AMXbooks 381, "An Ode to Dread." It was Christmas Day, 2017.

An Ode to Dread

To the world, he's Keith Eldred.
To me, he's just Dread.
I taught his son Ethan Spanish.
That's how we actually met.
Though at the time I'd been called "Spaniard,"
the name had been placed on the shelf.
My competition days were gone by.
For now, it was Teacher/Coach—nothing else.

See, Keith's always been creative,
but at the time I was not.
"There's this thing I want to do with you at the Library,
 he said.
"Sure, okay, let's give it a shot."
"I Challenge Charlie" was a moderate success indeed,
and it planted in me a creative seed.
As my fight career was winding down,
I didn't know what move to make.
"I'll help you write your book," Keith said.
"I know what it takes."
I learned very quickly that Keith was a sage.
A big book of wisdom without a last page.
In me, you hear him. His influence is strong.
Our mornings are very early. Our days are very long.
There's no way I could do this
without Dread by my side.
He sees me at my best and worst.
In him I do confide.
A virtuous man I've come to know.
With your belief in me, Dread,
to the top we will go.
What Spanish name was it, then,
that Ethan did choose?
"Incendio," it was. The definition, let's muse.
You give me your all without seeking a return,
because in me you see FIRE that will forever burn.

We can't stop believing

The Spaniard / World's Toughest Lifelong Learner vision makes sense to Dread and me despite the slow going. For whatever reason, or maybe better said, for so many odd and not-necessarily-connected reasons, we believe. We just can't quit.

One lesson I learned from fighting is: If you're ever to succeed, you need to have total self-belief and conviction. I've failed often in my life, and it feels much better to fail as a result of a decision that I made for myself vs. a decision that someone else made for me. I'll bet on me every time (See James Altucher's book *Choose Yourself*).

I study marketing expert Gary Vaynerchuk, and through his philosophies, I've become much more okay with learning to trust my gut. Simon Sinek, in his book *Leaders Eat Last*, elaborates on this idea, stating, "It is our limbic brain that feeds the gut reactions and gut decisions that drive our behavior." Too much rational thinking gets me flustered and indecisive. Just as in fighting, I do my best on feel. So call me limbic.

A thousand shovels a day with no return. It didn't matter. It had to work. It's pouring rain yet somehow you see sunshine.
Joe De Sena
Founder of Spartan
AMXtalks 70

What we runners were doing made no sense at all. Yet it made all the sense in the world.
Dean Karnazes
The Road to Sparta
AMXbooks 290

(On the quest to be the best and test limits) If this sounds arrogant, it's because it is. If you don't believe in your own greatness, no one else will.
Kevin Hart
I Can't Make this Up
AMXbooks 570

If you don't say and believe you're the best, who will?
Marc Mero
America's #1 School Presenter/Former WWE Champ
AMXtalks 152

The *How I Built This* podcast highlights the importance of the founders' belief while building a company. I specifically remember hearing about the evolution of Zumba and the Chipmunks. These things shouldn't have worked, but they did. Because the founders just kept going.

Phil Knight is quite possibly the most supreme example of sustaining belief and keeping on going. His book *Shoe Dog* opened my eyes up to what it really means to persevere. I took lessons from that book that guide me nearly every day.

15

What Guides Me

CONNECTION

A favorite practice I'd recommend employing: Identify people whom you aspire to be like, who could elevate you / your life, with whom you resonate strongly. Then set out to form a relationship with them.
Special episode from Echelon Front's Muster 005
AMXbooks 485

Success Principle #9 - Success Leaves Clues
Jack Canfield
The Success Principles
AMXbooks 424

Nothing shapes us more than the people around us. Early in life, most of this is by accident: You have no choice in who you are around, but eventually you can seek out the people you want to be around. Some, you can actually touch. Others, you can come to know in ways such as books, interviews and movies. Either way, you can choose to be around the people you want to be around. You can seek out people who can make a big difference.

That was crucial during my fight career. I sought out coaches, mentors and training partners. To steal a *Top Gun* line, I wanted to surround myself with "the best of the best," as thoroughly explained in *DRIVEN*.

Post-fighting, I understood the value of relationships, but it took on a different shape in this whole new world of business. I had already identified "Surroundings" as one of the Five Elements, but still, the relationship closest to home was my most important one.

A weird and still confusing topic to me is the idea of a supporting spouse. Try having the conversation late at night while you're lying in bed—justifying why you want to pursue professional fighting while it's risking your health and your family's welfare. Or maybe you lie there at night expressing your desire to pursue your dreams even though it's not moving your spouse's needle forward. She has her own hopes and dreams. She has her own wants and needs. Is it selfish of her to say, "I really wish you wouldn't fight because I'm worried about your long-term health and the risks that come along with it, but I don't want to be the one to tell you not to pursue your dreams."? What's the right answer? Is she supportive? Non-supportive? Kind of supportive?

I think I had a vision that there's this "all-in" mentality that, like Adrian, spouses are with you "no matter what." But even in Rocky's case, though Adrian was all-in, it was not without conflict. Reading *American Wife*, by Taya Kyle (wife of Chris Kyle, American Sniper), you see clear as day how this all plays out—one spouse supporting another spouse, but it never being easy. My current best explanation is that a spouse is non-supportive when he or she gives a finite ultimatum, if neither of you can come to a common ground. I think the conflict is just par for the course.

I have big dreams in the sense of impacting the world. Amanda has big dreams that are much closer to home. Together, we're figuring it out. Now consider your husband supporting another man's dreams with no current financial return. That's Dread's story. Amanda and Janet are fueling this ship and letting us be us.

Surround yourself with the best

"Surround yourself with the best" is one of the most powerful, repeated-in-my-head phrases by which I live. It is a mindset and mantra, and to clarify, "the best" is an idea, so don't go making the excuse, "Well, I don't have access to champions of the world, so I guess I'll just continue along this mediocre path." It's not only about surrounding yourself with actual champions of the world, it's about shaping the environment around you. It's gathering more and more good and getting rid of more and more bad.

When I decided I would become a UFC fighter, I knew I had to put everything into it. That meant leaving the comfortable spot I was living in. It meant moving away from friends and family, security in a full time job with a retirement plan and leaping into the unknown. At the time, I was a 26-year-old above-average former college wrestler who had been in one fight my entire life—when I was 12 or so and the recipient of typical junior high shenanigans. I had no real business making a declaration of one day fighting in the UFC. In my gut, I knew there was only one way to increase the odds of making it happen, and those chances were far from likely. I knew I had to surround myself with the best. I had to uproot myself and transplant myself into an environment that included the best fighters in the world. I needed to touch them, hear them, feel their energy and strength. I needed to know exactly what UFC fighters felt like and lived like, and I couldn't do it from Hollidaysburg, PA. I go in depth about the transition and surroundings in *DRIVEN*, but the major takeaway I want to emphasize here is the intentional decision of shaping my surroundings. To become the thing you want to become, you've got to surround yourself with it.

When I was young, my parents would put together every asset we had to send me to the best camps or to train with the best wrestlers. College was the same regarding wrestling and academics, and it continued on into the UFC. Post-UFC is where it got interesting, and that is a huge impetus for this book.

Not only should we consider the power of surroundings from our perspective, but we need to consider how we come off to others as well. Ben Askren (AMXtalks 104) is extremely successful. He's a multiple-time Division I national wrestling champion, an MMA champion, current UFC fighter, business owner and family man. He is someone who knows what he wants, speaks his mind and, like him or not, stays true to his values. Having seen him reach extreme levels of success in multiple areas of life, I wanted to learn from him.

He takes his coaching (Askren Wrestling Academy) extremely seriously and knows the impact that he has on those under his leadership. He said on my podcast (AMXtalks 104), "I have seen in my life, the difference a good coach and a bad coach can make in someone's life. Not just in their wrestling career, legitimately in their life. A great coach will give a kid a sense of belief in himself that's gonna last him for the next fifty years." Understand that you have the ability to surround yourself with the best, but you also have the ability to help other people surround themselves with the best. Be a valuable part of their surroundings. Consume energy from your environment and pass it right on to the next person.

I'll name just some of the people whose energy and knowledge I regularly absorb and want to pass on to you.

Frankie Edgar
UFC Champion

I clearly remember sitting in my Spanish classroom between classes thinking about what I wanted to do with my future. Surfing the internet, I saw that a college wrestling acquaintance, Frankie Edgar, had recently signed with the UFC. I write a lot about him and his influence on me in *DRIVEN*. I also interviewed him on my podcast, AMXtalks 24, the first interview I ever conducted for the show.

I want to drive home what I find to be the most important thing about Frankie. This is a quiet, blue-collar kid from South Jersey who rose to the absolute highest rank of professional fighting—world champion—overcoming obstacle after obstacle, living the underdog story as much as any person I've ever seen. He was undersized and overmatched in a vast majority of his fights on his way to the UFC title. It's difficult to encapsulate the awesomeness of Frankie Edgar in a few sentences. Through all that he has accomplished—the world titles, the travels, the money, the exposure—he is the same blue-collar kid from South Jersey that he was on Day 1. In our interview, when asked what it's like to be world champion, there's a smile in his voice when he says, "You come home, you're the world champ, and you still gotta change diapers." He went on to stress that "it takes a village," expressing gratitude to all of the people who have helped him along the way. Frankie Edgar is my North Star in deciding which road to take. I ask myself, "WWFD?"

Here's another way to say what Frankie has been to me. The idea comes from *How Adam Smith Can Change Your Life*, in which author Russ Roberts describes Scottish philosopher and economist Adam Smith's "Impartial Spectator." It's that thing inside of us that guides our actions and deems them moral or immoral. It's essentially our conscience. The Impartial Spectator is a collection of what we've learned from influences such as our parents, coaches and society, as well as our human nature. The Impartial Spectator is that thing that, the other night when my daughter was having a meltdown, made me think before I acted. "What would my Impartial Spectator think of how I am responding?" I asked myself.

Let's extend the idea of the Impartial Spectator beyond moral / immoral behavior and relate it to my surroundings while fighting professionally, and later we'll extend it into your surroundings. My Impartial Spectator basically became Frankie Edgar. What is Frankie doing? How is he approaching training? Who are his fighting influences? If he were here right now, would he choose to take the day off or would he make himself get to the gym to do what needs to be done? Those were the questions I asked myself and the measures on which I assessed myself. On top of everything, Frankie is a great person outside the cage, so his excellence mindset helped set the bar for me outside of fighting as well. A loyal listener sent me a quote yesterday from *The Daily Stoic*. It read, "Without a ruler to do it against, you can't make crooked straight." Frankie is my ruler. Who is yours?

I'm approaching ten years in the UFC. Still going at it. Still striving to get another title.
Frankie Edgar
UFC Champion
AMXtalks 24

Stitch Duran
Legendary Cutman

Another great example of someone in the combat sports world who lives their values is Jacob "Stitch" Duran. I mentioned him earlier related to parenting: His parents set him the kind of example that I hope to set for my kids. Stitch is one of the most famous / successful cutmen in the business. A cutman is the guy in the corner of a fight who tends to the bruises / cuts of the fighter in between rounds. I was fortunate to develop a relationship with Stitch over the years. He has worked with the best fighters in the world.

He has come a long way from being born and raised in a migrant camp. The address on his birth certificate is California Packing Company Camp Number 12. But he has not strayed at all from the values his parents modeled when he was a boy. "It's something I'm proud of. It wasn't based on economics, it was based on family and friendships. I was a farm worker. If you ate it, I picked it for you. Peaches, cotton, figs, apricots, tomatoes, I did it all. That's the only thing I knew, was how to give, how to work hard, and how to respect people."

"How to give, how to work hard and how to respect people ..." Those, my friends, are some core values, and Stitch lives them to this day. To drive this point home even further, on my trip to Madison Square Garden in New York City to watch Bellator in June 2017 with listener-turned-friend Lee, early in the night, before the fights, I saw Stitch from across the arena. He was making his way back into the tunnels that lead to the fighter area. He was working as a cutman at the event. I took out my phone and shot him a text. It read, "Hey brother! Section 108 mid way up. Row 9. Have fun! Looking good (fist-bump emoji)." From across the arena, I saw him take out his phone, stop, read the text, turn and look up to my section and then essentially bee-line it for where we were. He located us, jumped the rail, walked up the steps and sat down right next to us in one of the vacant seats. Mind you, Stitch is famous, especially in an arena full of fight fans. People were clamoring for pics, autographs—typical fan stuff—as he made his way toward us. He obliged with "Hellos" and handshakes as he made his way through the fans.

No one's better to have at your side than Stitch

A small, simple act of kindness and generosity like that can go a long way. We had developed a real relationship over the years, and it was important to him to talk to his friend. Part of this came from several years prior, at one of my fights

(UFC on Versus 6 in DC, I believe) when Stitch mentioned how cool my Spaniard shirts were. I ended up sending one to his daughter, and it's a gesture he never forgot. He said that it showed him what kind of person I was.

Marc Mero
Inspirational Speaker / Former WWE Champion

I was introduced to Marc Mero (AMXtalks 152), former WWE star, by way of Diamond Dallas Page (you've heard a little about DDP and will hear more soon). Marc had experienced extreme highs and lows during his life, including his tenure with the WWE. Drugs and personal loss plagued Marc's life for years, but he was able to turn things around and develop into America's #1 School Presenter. Marc was heavily influenced by DDP (another example of the importance of Surroundings) and leveraged his story into a completely new arena, professional speaking.

For over a decade, Marc has been traveling the country working non-stop to touch the lives of young people in need of reassurance and a positive message. His workload is absolutely incredible. He has done upwards of 300 presentations a year in recent years. My natural inclination: I want to learn from him. It's another opportunity to surround myself with the best. Marc is an extremely kind and helpful person, and he's gone out of his way to support my own speaking career, sharing all of his knowledge with no hesitation.

Marc's help has extended into all areas of professional speaking, but he said one thing in particular that stuck in my head. I've said it to myself nearly every day since. I even texted him to make sure that I got it exactly right. "If you don't say and believe you're the best, who will?" No one. The answer is no one will. Exercising accountability, you've got to take it upon yourself to BELIEVE you are the best, and one powerful way you do that is by surrounding yourself with the best.

Diamond Dallas Page
WWE Hall of Famer / Creator, DDPY

One of the neatest aspects of creating a podcast is the opportunity to speak to so many interesting people. Such is the case with WWE Hall of Famer Diamond Dallas Page (AMXtalks 111). I grew up watching wrestling (my brother was a super fan) and DDP's name had been around the industry for decades. He was best known for his wrestling career but has recently come out with DDP Yoga (or just DDPY), a full-body workout program that is a far cry from the traditional yoga that you and I are used to seeing / hearing about ("It ain't your mama's yoga" is his slogan). DDP and his yoga have transformed countless lives, including his friends and fellow superstars Jake "The Snake" Roberts and Scott Hall. He also happened to be my friend / fan / client Dave Wagner's wrestling hero.

I had heard from a few friends of mine that he is very personable and easily approachable, and we were eventually introduced via three-way email. Dave's birthday was coming up, so my intent was to ask DDP if he could give Dave a shoutout on social media. Not only did he respond, but it wasn't just a stock response—it was clear that DDP actually cared about Dave's transformation (losing 100 pounds) and was going out of his way to make Dave know that he respected his journey. Within the email exchange, DDP and I discussed his being on my show, and again, he went out of his way to make it happen in person. Coincidentally, DDP had an appearance at a local gym on a Saturday afternoon around this time, so Dave and I took the opportunity to meet him. I was scheduled to make the three-hour trip the day after the event to record the episode in person. DDP was on the east coast for a short time and fit me into his busy schedule. He actually invited me to his brother's house. I had asked his thoughts on Dave coming along for the ride, and he was all for it.

DDP, Dave and I sat and talked for close to two hours. We talked highs, lows, business, the wrestling business, Stone Cold, The Rock, Jake "The Snake" and more. The conversation was absolutely incredible. Thank goodness I have it recorded.

One of the most impactful things he said was, "Never underestimate the power you give someone by believing in them. Never underestimate the power you give yourself by believing in you." Again stressing accountability, you've got to own the way you interact with those around you. You've got to be aware of the things you say and do to the people around you. What power are you giving them by believing in them? What power are you taking away from them by NOT believing in them? The same goes for yourself. Be aware of the stories you tell yourself and others. Own it!

John Wooden
Late Great Coaching Legend

John Wooden is at the top of the list when it comes to purpose-DRIVEN, value-oriented people. Coach Wooden is one of the best coaches of all time across all sports. He won 10 national championships in 12 years, seven in a row, while coaching UCLA men's basketball. He is famous for attention to detail and teaching good habits that transcend the game of basketball. He never mentioned winning. In his book *Wooden on Leadership* he says, "The joy and great satisfaction I derived from leadership—working with and teaching others, helping them reach their potential in contributing to the team's common goals—ultimately surpassed outscoring an opponent, the standings, even championships." The standard Coach Wooden set for himself, and each individual on his team, was the standard that rippled outward from UCLA Basketball. Coach Wooden also goes on to distinguish one's reputation from one's character. He describes reputation as the perception of you by others, while character is who you truly are. In other words, your values add up to your character, so choose them wisely.

Scott Adams
Creator of "Dilbert"

Livestreaming podcast episodes is something that keeps me honest and systematic, though sometimes it seems no one is even watching. For this, I rely on Scott Adams, author and creator of the comic strip "Dilbert," whose book, *How to Fail at Almost Everything and Still Win Big*, has had a big influence on me. In it, he describes envisioning millions of people waiting ever so anxiously to read his soon-to-be-released book, and that he must finish it for them. That's the same mindset I've carried with me into AMXbooks every single morning. Though in reality, the amount of people tuning in to the actual livestream is minimal, and the amount of people who are anxiously awaiting my morning upload of that day's AMXbooks on my podcast feed is minimal, I treat it as though there are millions of people waiting in the wings, staring at their screens, butterflies in their bellies, holding their breath for the profound wisdom that is about to come their way. I don't care if it's true, and it doesn't matter. It's the belief that kickstarts me into action and keeps me accountable. I can trace this mindset back to fighting. The last thing in the world you want is to get tired in a fight, so you grow accustomed to accepting the fact that the other guy is pushing himself to extremes, spending every last ounce of his energy to dominate you in a fight, and that mindset drives you. It causes you to dig deep and find strength deep down inside of you that you never knew existed. You have no choice but to dig. He may be working harder than you, he may not be. But again, it doesn't matter. The belief drives the action. My belief that millions of people are anxiously awaiting my new day's original content drives me to prepare and deliver.

What has happened over the months is that I've developed relationships with a handful of daily viewers that I now know will be there every morning. They've told me they're anxiously awaiting the day's livestream, so I need to produce and execute for them. I also know that the only way I'm going to get to millions of people anxiously waiting in the wings is one person at a time.

16
What Guides Me

PREPARATION

(On Vince Lombardi's taking over as Green Bay Packers head coach) A thousand flits of fate could have taken him elsewhere, yet his entire football life seemed to have readied him for this moment.
David Maraniss
When Pride Still Mattered
AMXbooks 255

Your preparation is every day. Your preparation is how you life your life, such that when opportunity presents itself, you're ready.
AMXtalks 93

You want to be ready for opportunity. You want to be putting in the work now, because if you're sitting on your butt when it comes, you're gonna be like: I'm not ready for it. Honestly, not having opportunity is not as bad as having opportunity you can't take advantage of. That's the worst feeling in the world.
Andy Main
MMA Fighter / Business Owner
AMXtalks 95

(This was my commenting on the book) At one point, Bart Starr was benched. He chose to use his time wisely, such that he would be ready the next time his number was called. Ohio State coach Urban Meyer calls that competitive excellence—preparing so that if your number is called, you will be ready.
David Maraniss
When Pride Still Mattered
AMXbooks 261

Upon getting called for a potential acting gig, Boom Boom put the agent "on speakerphone so he could start banging out push-ups and sit-ups."
Mark Kriegel
The Good Son
AMXbooks 324

One of the strongest ways to improve your confidence is to dominate your preparation. When you know that you're prepared, you're going to feel more confident.
Dr. Cindra Kamphoff
Beyond Grit
AMXtalks 154

If you stay ready, you don't ever have to worry about getting ready.
Kevin Hart
I Can't Make this Up
AMXbooks 561

Repetition was at the core of Vince Lombardi's coaching philosophy. It would make his teams "fearless and instinctive."
David Maraniss
When Pride Still Mattered
AMXbooks 246

We were told long ago that the lion was king, that he is the most ferocious animal in the jungle. I agreed for the vast majority of my life: The lion is king. In the midst of this high-stakes journey I have chosen, though, I've begun to think differently. The lion is not king, Preparation is King.

You've heard the saying "Fatigue makes cowards of us all." Preparation and belief in what I'm pursuing have been my saviors when it comes to not fatiguing. I train my body and mind daily such that I'm able to perform when I'm called upon: Give a speech? Done. Fight somebody? Done. Climb a mountain? Done. Carry my kids for miles? Done. Preparation is how I live my life. I'm constantly priming my body and mind to be the best Spaniard I can be. It's not enough to talk about perseverance and hard work and commitment and lifelong learning, I've got to BE all of those things. When you think of sports excellence, names like Michael and Kobe and Lebron pop into your head. When you think of excellence in automobiles, what do you think of? My vision is that when you think of lifelong learning, the pursuit of something great, the no-quit attitude, hard work and sweat and perseverance, you think of The Spaniard.

The reason I never reached my potential as a wrestler, and the reason I came close to maximizing my potential as a fighter—it all came down to preparation. As a wrestler, I never truly knew what ultimate preparation looked like or felt like. As I matured, I was much more ready to hold myself accountable and truly put everything into preparation. The result was a clear mind primed for performance. I was able to let my skills do the talking. Anything less than ultimate preparation results in negativity and doubt, two enemies of maximum performance.

Confidence can be such a tricky thing ... if you let it be.

I've learned to simplify it, though. If you can look around the room and can then look at yourself in the mirror and truly believe you have worked harder than the competition, you will be confident. Period. Take that "but" and shove it. A few months ago, I read a Frankie Edgar tweet that went something like this: "If you're worried about getting tired, you aren't training hard enough." That's about as much truth as one can have.

My confidence in speaking and podcasting comes from learning. It comes from repetition and practice. It comes from waking up early, reading, studying, learning and extracting the most powerful, relatable learning points, penning them to paper and teaching them with little-to-no turnaround time. It forces me to hone my craft. I have no choice but to speak clearly, intelligently, relatably and entertainingly. It's now second nature (after having produced 1000+ episodes of my podcast) to be able to roll with it if I forget what I'm saying in front of a live audience and have to think on my toes, or quite possibly pivot in a completely different direction, all the while in a manner that gives off no sign. You can only do that when you have a matrix of information stored in your noggin, waiting to be extracted from at a time that neither you nor anyone else can predict.

I'm winning and losing on a daily basis in a relatively low-risk environment while developing my craft. Livestreaming is not easy. Cold-calling while livestreaming is not easy, and doing 1000 push-ups in 34 minutes while livestreaming is not easy (both of which I've done on Facebook Live), but all these little pieces, in addition to my AMX episodes, interviews, presentations and workshops, add up to confidence. I aim to be the most sought-after speaker / entertainer in the world. In ancient Greek society, people used to go to philosophy lectures as if they were sporting events or concerts. That's what I'm after. I want to bring back the lecture, but make it so entertaining that no one ever thinks of it as a lecture.

My history with preparation

I'll cover this in a few different areas: Wrestling, studies, *Pros vs. Joes* and fighting.

Wrestling. Wrestling is the type of sport that demands the highest levels of mental and physical preparation possible for success. It might not make sense to say the preparation required to be a world-class wrestler surpasses that of professional fighting, but I believe it does. I haven't quite put my finger on how or why, but nothing on Earth I've done thus far has been more mentally or physically challenging than wrestling.

Studies. Repetition and consistency have allowed me to succeed in every academic setting I've entered. It's too bad, at those various times throughout my life, that I didn't see the bigger picture of learning. I was just out to get good grades and pass. It took my decades of schooling and lots of maturing to see the bigger picture.

"Pros vs. Joes." I took on this reality show competition as if it were a national championship match / world championship fight. To me, that's how high the stakes were. I believe wholeheartedly I outprepped everyone, and that is why I won.

Fighting Rick Story. Either you have read about it already or could read all about it in *DRIVEN*. This victory and life-changing moment was the direct result of preparation, and multiple levels of preparation at that: Not only leading up to the fight but during fight week as well. My initial fight had been called off, but I stayed the course, maintained my normal fight week preparation and ended up defeating the #6 ranked fighter in the world.

Stories about preparation from the podcast

Todd Orr
Survivor of a Grizzly Bear Attack
AMXtalks 128

I had the opportunity to interview grizzly-bear-attack-survivor Todd Orr (AMXtalks 128), whose preparation and level-headed thinking played a key role in his survival. He was ready when he needed to be. Here are a few things he said in the interview:

I'm used to practicing pulling bear spray out and being ready to spray if I need to. Just run that through your head and be aware of the situation that you're in.

It's going back to having some training, reading about it, having some classes, knowing what a bear's capable of and what you can and can't do against them.

(While being chewed on by the bear) I kept telling myself over and over, "Don't move, she's gonna leave. Don't make a sound." I was prepared, knowing, "You've got to do this, or you're gonna die." It was just the will to survive.

Being in that situation and having a bear pin you to the ground chewing on you—it was not fun. It was very scary, and I thought I was gonna die, and I would hate to see someone else go through that. I felt I was really lucky. It could have been so much worse.

Ariel Helwani
World's Leading MMA Journalist
AMXtalks 72

A friend of mine who also happens to be one of the top journalists in mixed martial arts (MMA), Ariel Helwani taught me a thing or two about the power of a vision and preparation. Ariel was prepping to be the leading MMA journalist before MMA even went mainstream. And guess what? He's now the leading face of MMA journalism on ESPN!

I first met Ariel when we were both young in our careers. I was living in New Jersey, and he was located in New York City. Simply being close to him probably led to the development of our relationship. Add to the fact that we both cry a lot, love our kids immensely and talk easily, and we have a lot in common. Early in his career, he needed content, and I was willing and able to help provide a portion of it, so we clicked. Beyond that, we became friends. He is one of the purest, most authentic people I've met in the game. As soon as I started my show, it was a foregone conclusion that I wanted to have him on, and he didn't bat an eye when I asked him (AMXtalks 72). He's a busy guy with a lot of responsibilities, so I was especially grateful for the opportunity.

The first thing I think of when reflecting on that interview was vision (you'll see why shortly), so I could have used him as an illustration in my earlier section about vision. But I want to point out how even an exciting vision goes nowhere without putting in the work. If you see yourself a certain way in the future, you've got to prepare to become that person. That's exactly what Ariel did. Early in our conversation he described his strategy for differentiating himself from other up-and-coming sports reporters in journalism school:

I noticed that everyone there wanted to be the same thing—the baseball / basketball / football guy.
This was 2001, before the Ultimate Fighter boom—the UFC was only eight years old. I remember telling my parents, "In ten years, this sport of mixed martial arts is going to be mainstream, and there's probably going to be an executive in some office saying, 'Okay, we have to start covering this. Who's the guy?' I want to put myself in a position to be The Guy." The crazy thing about that is, 2011, exactly 10 years later, is when I got my job at Fox. The UFC gets this deal with Fox, and they go, "Okay, who's the Insider Guy?"

Note: Later, when Fox's contract with the UFC expired, Ariel became "The Insider Guy" on ESPN.

That. Is. Foresight! That is having a vision! That is preparation. Ariel saw himself being the Insider Guy. He did everything he had to do to put himself in the position of being identified as The Guy. Of course, you've got to stay present and live in the here and now, but you've also got to have that carrot dangling out in front of you to know what the heck you're fighting for. And the way to fight for it is preparation.

I look at my everyday as preparation. For what? Life. I'm preparing to be a physically and mentally well-oiled machine that is ready for whatever comes my way. In essence, I'm training for everything, kind of. To actually prepare for everything is impossible. There are too many variables and possibilities. But you can prepare the tools you will call upon when dealing with whatever comes your way: Your mind and your body. Most simply put, read books and exercise daily. That's the essence of lifelong learning: Broadening your knowledge and capabilities so that you're better prepared for any developments that arise during each and every day.

An interesting thing happens when you read so many books: You see patterns and commonalities across the spectrum of life. You're able to infer and learn from other people's experiences that more or less fit within a common set of categories. It's like you develop a database of examples to call upon when in need. Have you ever heard of mental reps? Reading books is performing mental reps, both in the short-term and long-term. You're training your mind with books while you're training your body with weights and movement. That combo prepares you to fight the day. There's no escaping trouble. It will find you. You have a choice: train for it or don't train for it. Might training be a waste of your time? Highly doubtful. If you're the one person on Earth to whom only good things come, and you never need to use any of the things you learn, consider it a gain that you got more out of your faculties than you otherwise would have.

Patrick Murphy
Former U.S. Under Secretary of the Army
AMXtalks 68

If you think bad things will never happen to you, that you'll never be called upon to be ready, here's a great example of how my friend Patrick Murphy's physical training made him ready to help others during a life-and-death emergency. He told the story on AMXtalks 68.

First a little background: Patrick recalls throwing himself into fitness, including morning P90X workouts during his days in the U.S. Congress. But after leaving Congress, he completed a 5K in a time that disappointed him, so he investigated CrossFit training near his home. During the initial evaluation, he was embarrassed at underperforming yet again, especially on the rope climb, unable to complete even one rep. After months of faithful effort pushing himself, he reached a point of completing 21 rope climbs in one routine workout. At this time, in May 2015, he was also approaching his Senate confirmation hearing to be named United States Under Secretary of the Army. That evening, he was on an Amtrak train heading home from DC, and that train was involved in an accident in Philadelphia. Tragically, eight people were killed. Patrick was in the third car and was thrown from one end to the other and knocked unconscious. All around him were debris and blood and people's cries. After regaining consciousness and recalling where he was, he saw the moon through the open window above him and set about helping those around him. As if completing a rope climb, he was able to pull himself up to reach the emergency window and open it so that everyone could get out. His doctor told him that his strong neck helped him avoid death or paralysis. In our interview, he said, "I'm not saying everybody should do CrossFit. Everybody has a different path to succeed and work out and carry themselves like a champion. That happens to be my workout. I know that I've been very, very lucky. Sometimes you make your own luck by working hard, but I've been very blessed. I don't know what the next chapter is, but I know I'm going to do it with a smile on my face and with a clear mind and a clear heart."

This goes directly back to the old saying, "Luck is when preparation meets opportunity." Patrick was prepared. For what? Life. In this particular instance, it happened to be a physical feat to which he was called. As a friend of such a highly successful person, I've seen first-hand how he lives his life. It's very detailed and systematic. He lives like a professional.

My preparation for wrestling and fighting required me

to be at a peak physical and mental state. It was rather straightforward: I had the baddest dudes on the planet waiting to smash my face in if I didn't perform. That's enough to make you put in the extra rep and steer clear of the junk food. There was a direct cost related to NOT preparing to my utmost, and that cost hurt ... really badly.

My preparation for speaking and podcasting is no less important, though it is different in that no one is chomping at the bit to kick my a**. There is no ginormous tiger in the room licking his lips, waiting to pounce. This lack of pressure could cause me to let my guard down a bit. I mean, no one's waiting to smash my face, so what if I sleep in? So what if I skip a workout and eat garbage? I could go that way, but I don't. I hold myself to a higher standard, one that was ingrained by my parents. I know what it's like to fear having the baddest dudes on the planet smash my face in if I don't perform, and frankly, that's enough to make me never want to under-prepare for anything ever again. And by under-prepare, I mean give anything less than my absolute best.

The preparation for speaking and podcasting comes from both my life experiences, and from the acts of speaking and podcasting. My natural inclination to enjoy being on stage (wrestling mat / cage / actual stage) helped draw me to my current profession, but that's only the beginning. If we go back a few paragraphs to how I live my life, I'm preparing myself every day by reading books, asking questions, thought-exploring, reasoning (in my head and with others), and training. I'm chipping away daily to become the best Spaniard possible, so, in essence, to whatever I direct my energies, I'll be doing it to the best of my abilities.

I livestream AMXbooks every day so I get used to being in front of a live audience. I can't start over or hit stop. I intentionally talk so much on live camera to get used to talking in front of people live. You can't just say whatever you want without thought. You have to consciously consider what words come out of your mouth. The stakes are higher when there's a live audience. Over time, this has developed my ability to formulate thoughts into words, balance the line between "say this or don't say this" and recall information off the cuff. My AMX system of learning is very intentional. Over time, the data I consume is either stored and recalled directly or stored and saved, indirectly helping to form the words that are coming out of my mouth.

I have a passion for asking questions, or maybe you could call it an obsession, and when I'm in a conversation to learn, I'm all ears. I look at it as an adventure: Two people settling down to explore the frontiers of each other's minds / experiences, as well as the new frontier that results as a combination of the two. There's no set protocol or guide that tells you when to push further, when to ask a follow-up question, when to back off slightly or completely, when to wait it out and let your guest continue even though a silence commences / lingers or what subjects to bridge, and that is what I love about the craft of interviewing. I limit my amount of direct research for each guest because I love the anticipation and excitement of leaving myself open to surprise (sometimes embarrassment) and exploration.

I have a passion for creating powerful conversations that impact people at the most core / basic / primal level of being human. I've facilitated and been part of environments in which words and conversation affect people dramatically. Creating this type of conversation and environment is a special opportunity that I'll never take for granted. I'm told I have a natural gift for interviewing, and I'm told I continue to improve. The first may be luck or genetics, but the second, the improvement, is a result of diligent study and repetition. There is no substitute for putting in the time and reflecting on that time with the intent to improve.

The interviews I'm especially glad I was ready for

During interviews, you never know what is going to come up. Sometimes the moments are sensitive or so important that they deserve careful treatment. It's essential that I'm ready and have a passion for listening and for guiding the conversation. I'm glad that I can bring skill and expertise to every talk, but there were particular moments that really made me glad I had made myself ready.

Ashleigh Williamson
Rebuilder of Her Own Life
AMXtalks 83

In the heyday of my career, when things were at their peak, I'd do various fan events across a handful of states, mostly in PA and NJ. Every once in a while, I'd travel a few more hours than normal, but the vast majority were within my usual circle and relatively low-key. There was one, though, where the UFC brought me to Philly as a "guest fighter." That meant they wined and dined me and Amanda and showcased me to fans at various events leading up to that weekend's UFC event. It was a way of promoting up-and-coming fighters. This was between my victory against Rick "The Horror" Story (who was #6 in the world at the time) and Anthony "Rumble" Johnson (who is agreed upon as the scariest man in the UFC). For a minute, I was hot stuff!

On the other side of the glitz and glamour of the big-time events were local events in my hometown area of Central PA. People I didn't know or hadn't seen in forever would come by and make small talk. It was nice, and it was humbling that (1) a bar / restaurant would pay me to come sit and talk to people, and (2) people would actually come talk to me. Mind you, there weren't always a lot of people. But one of the fans who always came to my events back home was Ashleigh Williamson. She was quiet and reserved. The first time I remember seeing her, she was seated in the back by herself, the first one to arrive. That in itself was pretty bold. I invited her to sit with us, and it turned out she worked at the same company as my brother. A connection was made.

Over the years, Ashleigh and I became friends. Our spouses met, and eventually our kids met. She's a super-nice person who showed me support from Day 1, and for that I'm grateful. She's done great photography work for me and my family, and we've combined our skills (hers in photography, and mine in … well, I'm still figuring it out!) to create a goodwill event at which Ashleigh took professional pictures for free, and I delivered my love-of-learning talk. It was a bold move that we, along with Dread, made together. We had a seed of an idea—"Let's do good for people"—that turned into an event.

I tell you all of this to set up, quite possibly, the most unexpected sentence someone has ever said to me. I knew Ashleigh hadn't had the easiest life, and that there were areas where she was still battling. Through our friendly conversation and our formal work together, a bit more of it had come out. I always tried to stay the course in helping her through her challenges while also respecting the fact that I was relatively new and inexperienced in working with people one-on-one. Months after our coaching sessions, I asked Ashleigh to be on my show. She had inside knowledge of my career that would be interesting for others to hear, but she also had an incredible story: A regular person who is not only dealing with her challenges head-on, but thriving. She has a healthy, beautiful family, a good job and another passionate budding profession in photography. She is the epitome of the message that I am trying to send.

Yet this is what she said on my podcast, describing a moment as a young adult, the lowest point of her entire life:

It was the taste of the metal of the barrel of the gun in my mouth that made me say, what the hell am I doing? That's not the answer. From that moment in the bathroom on that floor, I just knew that there was something out there waiting for me, and I just had to be patient and find it, and I did. I feel like the phoenix rising from the ashes.

"It was the taste of the metal of the barrel of the gun in my mouth ..."

My jaw dropped. I was absolutely speechless. I fight people for a living. I voluntarily lock myself in a cage to fist fight another trained man. But when Ashleigh said that, I felt as ill-equipped as I ever had before. I could not even fathom what that was / is like. My respect for her, already extremely high, turned into straight admiration. The strength that she showed then, and now, talking about it for others to learn from, was a moment in my life I will never forget. And one of the boldest moves anyone in my circle has ever made. I'm just glad that I had enough interviews and live experience and reps under my belt to keep listening and asking questions to bring out Ashleigh's important story.

Desiree Magee
Mitochondrial Disease Parent / Expert
AMXtalks 195

Desiree is married to Rich Magee, one of my best friends in junior high. He's an extremely successful guy who comes from an extremely successful family. I'm fortunate to have met and spent time with all of them. As we grew up, we grew apart, but we never lost the connection that was so strong at one time. It's like we hold a special place in each other's memories because we know that at one time we had such prominent roles in the other's life. Post-high school and -college, we'd see each other at holiday time, random trips to who-knows-where for who-knows-what and at some of my fight cities. Rich ended up marrying Desiree and moving out west to California. Their daughter Daphne was born with Mitochondrial Disease, which affects her energy and strength levels. She's the most beautiful little girl, and watching her / their fight against the disease is both inspiring and heart-wrenching. They are special people.

On one of our random trips to who-knows-where for who-knows-what (a bachelor party in Denver, actually), Rich brought up the idea of having Desiree on the show as part of Mitochondrial Disease Awareness Week. I was all in. This is the exact type of conversation I want to have. It's inspiring, educational, informative, empathy-building, real and very difficult to traverse. Rich and Desiree are my friends, but I was extremely worried about saying the wrong thing, unintentionally offending Desiree and their family. I was toeing a very delicate line.

I learned quickly that Desiree was super helpful and welcoming in the face of all my concerns. This was one of the most memorable and valuable conversations I've ever had. If you can get through my sobbing noises in the episode, you will hear the magic of conversation that I spoke of earlier. It was truly an example of the primalcy and beauty that comes along with being human. We were two people connected by friendship who explored some of the most difficult scenarios and conversations life can present. Here are some segments from our talk:

> You can't sit down and just be like, "Oh, woe is me, my world is so horrible" and let it consume you. You have to get back up, you have to fight, you have to become the best advocate for your child, you have to figure out the best treatment, the best doctors. Time is of the essence.

> A lot of my friends will say, "You were made for this." Well, I don't think so. I don't think I am any more capable of handling this than the next person. I think it's in everyone. I think certain situations will bring it out of you, whether it's wrestling, or a child with an illness ... or adult co-ed league soccer, and I'm going to fight through it! I think everyone does have it. It just takes that one thing to pull it out of them.

> We do need to reset ourselves sometimes. Not all families survive through situations like this. At the end of the day you have to be a normal family. Your child has to be able to do normal things. You've got to keep a relationship with your spouse, and you've got to keep the core values of what made you you. Otherwise the disease will totally consume everybody.

> The sibling of a special needs child has a warmer heart than almost anyone. She's far stronger than I am [Adelaide, Daphne's older sister]. Both my kids are, actually. She is literally the light of her sister's eyes. She

is ours as well. We're so proud of everything that she does, even when she's difficult! Because she pushes us, even though she might not be aware, to be the best versions of us—just to be normal. It's just incredible to be the parent of a child like her.

A key principle about preparation

Rule #4 - Compare Yourself to Who You Were Yesterday, Not to Who Someone Else is Today
Jordan Peterson
12 Rules for Life
AMXbooks 458

One of the most problematic habits in my life has been worrying about everyone else—how well *they* are doing, how much *their* contract is worth, what the coach thinks of *them*, how much better I could do if I were in *their* spot. It's taken a lot of introspection to realize that for much of my life, I was playing a zero-sum game. In my distorted, deepest, loneliest and most fearful self, I would see someone else's win as my loss. A totally self-centered way of thinking. My perspective was that of victim (woe is me) and deficit (there's not enough good to go around). It was an outward projection of the insecurities I felt inwardly. It's not that I'm totally cured today, but I'm much more aware. If you ever find yourself stuck in that distorted train of thought and need a quick reminder, this quote has helped me: "All ships rise in a high tide." Remember there IS enough good to go around.

It's really tough for me to be honest about this, as it's one of my least favorite parts about myself, but part of this entire process (developing my business and identity) is fully learning about and understanding myself and sharing what I learn. I'm embarrassed to say that in my misery, I enjoyed company. I was so doubtful of succeeding in my biggest endeavors that I would assume I'd fall short, and when anyone else did too, I'd welcome them to a seat right next to me. I found comfort in sharing my sorrows. If they lost, it took the pressure off me. That goes all the way back to my senior year state final wrestling match. Earlier in the tournament, my teammate won the state title in his weight class. Leading up to my match, in my mind, I had already lost. "Great, he won. Now I'll lose. Doesn't it just figure?" He and I were always head-to-head growing up, and that mindset is what damned me at many of my most important competitive moments.

It's a day-to-day process overcoming these "healthy pathological" thoughts (as Dread puts it... healthy because they result in a net positive and don't hold me back). My new ideal is such that (when I'm at my best) I don't consider for one second what he / she / everyone else is up to.

This is something I've become much more aware of and focused on overcoming in its entirety. It wasn't until much later in life, during my UFC career, when losses meant months of wallowing in sorrow, that I began to evolve and see that there is much more to competition (and life) than winning.

I came across this quote while reading Russ Roberts' *How Adam Smith Can Change Your Life*, and it stuck:

> *Baal Shem Tov, Jewish mystic and founder of the Hasidic movement, says, "We notice the flaws in those around us to remind us of our own flaws and to spur us to self-improvement."*
> **Russ Roberts**
> **How Adam Smith Can Change Your Life**
> *AMXbooks 395*

17

What Guides Me

SERVICE

One day the games/matches/fights/contests will end (or at the very least evolve), and it truly is about being a good person. This makes me think of the extremely entertaining and easily digestible book *Legacy* by James Kerr, which details the culture and leadership principles of New Zealand's All Blacks professional rugby team, one of the most successful sports teams in the world. Kerr lays down one of their principles simply as "No dickheads," followed up by "Better people make better All Blacks." Become a better person, and you will become better in whatever capacity you are living.

Imagine the ripple effect you can have on the people around you simply by working hard and being kind and considerate of others. A friend and former guest on my show, business leader / musician / athlete Lee Witt, said, "When we walk in our front door after work, when we go to our office in the morning, we can make conscious decisions to actually make that a better environment. It can be up to us, and we can take that on ourselves and our responsibility to go: 'I'm going to change the energy of this room.'" He went on to describe this simple idea as "elevating the room."

Look, I didn't always get this, and I don't always remember it. I've spent plenty of my life (mostly when I was younger, or at least I like to think so) operating in a mode of Me Me Me. I would look at certain jobs and wonder, "How can they be happy? That's not fun at all. I want to have fun." By contrast, I came to realize that any work can be enjoyable, or at least meaningful, and so can any life. It's about spending yourself in a cause that is greater than yourself, leading a school, leading a business, creating or providing a product. I was served a dose of humility and self-awareness.

Success Principle #62 - Find a Way to Serve
Jack Canfield
The Success Principles
AMXbooks 442

Perhaps service and sacrifice are the dues we pay for living.
James Hunter
The Servant
AMXboooks 453

I have a list of 100 things that I'm trying to do to be happier in life, and it's morphed into this helping platform.
Sebastian Terry
Adventurer & Inspirationalist
AMXtalks 177

Be a Volunteer - It pays naturally into the life philosophy that to get, you have to give.
Bear Grylls
A Survival Guide for Life
AMXbooks 506

Gary Vee says a successful entrepreneur shares three characteristics: Commitment to service, desire to provide value, love of teaching.
GaryVaynerchuk
Crushing It!
AMXbooks 420

I want to help. I even have a natural impulse to help. When I was a kid, and I'd walk past "Help Wanted" signs in store fronts, I'd always think to myself, "Aww, I wish I had money to give them." I thought they needed money. I came to learn later they were looking for workers. One of the things Dread has helped me realize is that you can set up a structured approach to ensure you are helping others. For one person, it might be giving money every week at church. Someone else might take a regular shift at the animal shelter. You don't have to think about doing good, because it's already on your calendar / in your budget.

I've tried to make *The Spaniard Show* a structure like that. From the word go, the show is built to help others. First of all my kids, as I've discussed. And the books I pick and the interviews I do are ones where I find value. I extract the gold from these books and pass it on to others.

I've said that sometimes Dread believes in me even more than I do myself, and he often sees more good in me than I do, more good in what I'm doing. So the rest of this chapter is him talking. When I'm asked for a favorite quote, I often reference something my dad told me when I was young: "Don't going around telling people how good you are, let them tell you." I've thought of that mainly related to wrestling / sports performance, but right now I mean what I've been talking about: Doing good and helping others.

I'll shut up and let Dread talk.

DREAD SPEAKS

Whew, I thought he would never step aside. This is Dread. I do have good things to say about Spanny, and not just to puff him up. It's because serving others is essential in having a satisfying life, and that's what all of this is about. If using himself as an example brings him too much uncomfortability, fine. I'll do it. It's simply convenient to use The Spaniard as an example of helping others because we can keep talking about the podcast and his talks as illustrations.

Here are some of the ways that I see The Spaniard as having been of great service:

He's highlighted members of the military

Neither Spanny nor I joined the military, but both of our fathers did, and Spanny's oldest brother Scott did, and we have the highest respect for service members. In *DRIVEN*, Spanny expresses his deep satisfaction at taking part in UFC events and initiatives that specially honored the troops, including a tour of the Middle East. As of this writing, Spanny's 120+ guests have included 18 U.S. veterans, and during episodes, he frequently highlights lessons from books written by and / or about veterans or service members, including *Extreme Ownership, American Wife, Mikey and the Dragons, The Dichotomy of Leadership, Way of the Warrior Kid, Team Dog* and *Make Your Bed*. By my calculation, at least 10% of the Spaniard's time and attention goes toward the military. Also, during the holiday season of 2017, a Spaniard live event offering free portrait photos by Ashleigh Williamson collected monetary donations for the Hollidaysburg Veterans Home.

He's shown a heart for kids

That has shone through in the book already, as The Spaniard has discussed his own kids, his appearances in schools, and his commitment to AMXkids episodes. I just wanted to share a few more specifics that I've gotten to witness up close. I got to see him go into great detail advising a teenage martial artist and prospective professional fighter who hung around after an event. I've seen him stress to kids that he, the professional fighter, has experienced (and still does experience) great amounts of fear and self-doubt and that he was bedeviled by bullies as a student and beset even as an adult by online trolls. Imagine the impact on them of hearing things like that from someone like him. Here is a story that Spanny shared in a Facebook post:

A Small Yet Courageous Act

I was fortunate to speak at two different high schools yesterday (Portage / Central Cambria, PA), spreading a message of "fight." Not the kind I did in a cage, rather the kind we are all faced with on a daily basis: Is fighting for what I really want / believe in really worth the struggle? Do I have the strength / will / fortitude to see it through, or should I take the easy road? Should I cash in my chips and settle for less than my best? OR do I fight tooth and nail and go out on my shield?

While I had a multitude of powerful connections throughout the day, one in particular sticks in my mind. Following my presentation, amidst a group of energetic high schoolers, a girl approached me from the side. I saw her coming from the corner of my eye and turned to greet her. At this point, there were probably 25 high school students in my vicinity.

She took a moment, collected her thoughts, and started to speak. She hesitated, then continued on, talking about one of the books I mentioned during my talk. She had read it, and we began to go in depth about it. She was visibly nervous, as most young people are when talking to adults. But shortly into our conversation, she paused for more than a few seconds. She was very uncomfortable, extremely nervous, so I put her at ease, expressing, "It's okay, take your time."

She was silent for 10 seconds. Her uncomfortability increased. Then she slowly started to say (paraphrased), "I'm very sorry. I have social interaction anxiety. This is very hard for me to do." (I, Charlie, actually shed a tear just now thinking about it).

I briefly talked with her about her anxiety and then brought the focus back onto the book. My thought was that the familiarity and comfort with the book would put her at ease. It did. We finished our brief interaction.

Prior to saying goodbye, I expressed how proud I was of her for fighting through that anxiety and struggle, for putting herself into a group of 25 energetic students to interact with me. It would have been easier for her to not approach me, not talk about the book and go on her way.

Chills. Am I right, people?

(This was my commenting on the book) Ever feel like an Outsider? Me, too. My guess is everyone else has, too.
S.E. Hinton
The Outsiders
AMXkids 13

He's shown a heart for the
intelectually and physically disabled

One of The Spaniard's most special mutual fan clubs is students with intellectual disabilities attending college through Pennsylvania's D.R.E.A.M. Partnership. Spanny has held multiple workshops for these students. In the same vein, one of his most inspiring podcast guests was Matt Marcinek (AMXtalks 88) a jiu-jitsu competitor with cerebral palsy who competes against able-bodied athletes and who won his first match after 80 tries and ten years. Add in episodes featuring injured veterans: Matt Bradford (AMXtalks 190, whose motto is "No legs, no vision, no problem"), Earl Granville and Jonathan Lopez (AMXtalks 132), both amputees active with Operation Enduring Warrior (a Veteran Service Organization). And as you have read, one of his most touching conversations was with Desiree Magee, battling for the health of her daughter. One more example that has all of my own heart: You've already heard The Spaniard mention my own wife's diagnosis of dementia. I have seen firsthand that The Spaniard's podcast is a welcoming platform for sharing information about a range of disabilities and special needs.

He has highlighted natives of his hometown

The Spaniard has amazed me by regularly featuring remarkable guests who happen to be friends from his youth. It reflects well on the town of Hollidaysburg that one small circle includes so many achievers. It's the kind of thing that could end up attracting new, active, hopeful residents. Is *The Spaniard Show* a recruiting tool for this area? To a degree, yes! And that is yet another service. Here are the guests I have in mind, along with the original descriptions that I wrote when we published their episodes.

Jack Zerby
Passionate Musician, Designer, Digital Entrepreneur
AMXtalks 85
Talk about touching the big time ... or being only one or two degrees away. This episode's guest discusses connections to Citibank, Saks Fifth Avenue, Jon Stewart, Martha Stewart, the New York Jets, Rihanna, Nike, Johnson & Johnson, Apple, Microsoft, Sprint, College Humor, Vimeo, Tumblr, Bleacher Report, Uber, Maker-Bot and Etsy. Oh, plus Facebook and Mark Zuckerberg himself! This guest will guide our minds from East Coast to West Coast and help us imagine millions of dollars flowing about while going for broke pursuing personal passions.

Matt Anderson
Emmy-Winning Film Editor
AMXtalks112
The Spaniard owes Matt big-time for creating his website and designing his T-shirts during his fight career. But you'll see that these were labors of love that go back to their school days. It's crazy fun to hear them look back on pizza lunch and that time with the rattlesnake. Plus hearing Matt's stories about Channing Tatum, Matthew Broderick, Amy Adams ... consuming all the wrong things before and during marathons ... bluffing his way into Oakland Arena ... and just plain taking leaps of faith and pursuing what he loves. Which, oh by the way, led the guy to win an Emmy!

Matt Furman
Leading Photographer
AMXtalks 134
Matt Furman knows how to deliver a powerful photo. Just look at his striking "Mouthpiece Pic" of The Spaniard. And visit furmanfoto.com to see the drama

he finds whether photographing the unsung or the world-famous (hello, Wayne Gretzky and Ivanka Trump!) What are the chances that Matt is yet another member of The Spaniard's hometown circle? Yup. Listen to these two hometownies talk family, freelancing and framing world-class images. (Addendum: Also on Matt's website are images of John Legend, Neil Young, Mira Sorvino, Laird Hamilton, Ronan Farrow, Janelle Monae, Mariano Rivera, Graham Nash ...)

Erik Lilla
Go-Getting Gymnastics Guru
AMXtalks 92

Who woulda predicted that a grade-school wrestling pal of The Spaniard's in Pennsylvania would wind up in Nebraska? Much less become a high school valedictorian, a 4.0 Engineering major, then owner with his wife of a gymnastics training center with two locations and hundreds of students? This is a fascinating review of how Erik Lilla has passionately pursued goals all of his life and continues to dream big.

Rich Magee
Plasma Physicist
AMXtalks 203

By popular demand, this episode explores physics in general and string theory in particular. Okay, it wasn't exactly like that. The truth is that after reading a book on astrophysics, The Spaniard had questions for Rich Magee, a pal since boyhood who just happens to be a plasma physicist. So strap in for the podcast's first mentions of such matters as fusion reaction, a little something that Rich is working on to help all of humanity. [NOTE: Rich is married to Desiree, mentioned earlier in the book.]

Ray Boom Boom Mancini was an agent of hope and belief for Youngstown, OH. He came around at the right time for a city in need of something.
Mark Kriegel
The Good Son
AMXbooks 318

He shares everything he's learning

Before I turn the book back over to The Spaniard, I want to underline what he is doing for his family, for me, and, as I see it, for you as well—for anyone, as the Bible says, "who has ears to hear and eyes to see." He is showing the way to get what you want, in any area: Emotions, relationships, savings, skills, fitness, appearance, anything. Because he points to the knowledge and wisdom all around us in people, books and institutions that open up every corner of existence to the limit that anyone has explored it. It is said that in a time when information is so readily available, ignorance is a choice. Will you choose to know how to help yourself? Or at least how to try? That is what I see The Spaniard asking every day. It's an ongoing challenge to me, and I pass on the challenge to you.

Another word on TRYING to help yourself. As I write this, The Spaniard and I have not cracked the code on how to build his career and help as many people as we want to. In that sense, we have not succeeded. But we are trying, and we are learning more every day about trying. I could not ask for a better partner or example of applying the very practices he talks about in this book: Perseverance, Boldness, Consistency, just to highlight a few. It is an honor to struggle beside him, to be entrusted with his doubts, and to see him always keep on keeping on. Back to you, Spaniard.

I always used to say to the younger fighters: Look what Charlie does. Look what Jim and Dan do. If you want to be that, you gotta do what they do. It would be that way with anything. If you want to be a successful baseball player, look at Derek Jeter. Look what he did. Look at his work ethic. You gotta follow the guys that have laid the path and gotten there before you.

Dr. Tom
Chiropractor / MMA Sponsor
AMXtalks 96

18
TAKING ACTION

How I use my new and lasting system

A system is "something you do on a regular basis that increases your odds of happiness in the long run."
Scott Adams
How to Fail at Almost Everything and Still Win Big
AMXbooks 354

Today's new book gives "twelve profound directives for living properly within the order and chaos of our lives."
Jordan Peterson
12 Rules for Life
AMXbooks 454

Success seems at times an imaginary creature, impossible to capture.
Scott Alexander
Rhinoceros Success
AMXbooks 516

*I think the vast majority of extraordinarily successful
people follow the same blueprint.*
Colonel Tim Nye
**Marine / Soldier / Member of the Spartan Up! Podcast
Team**
AMXtalks 129

*(Quote from John Wooden) There are no big things,
only the accumulation of little things.*
Daniel Coyle
The Talent Code
AMXbooks 181

I mentioned early in this book that my system
has evolved and that something else now takes front seat to
The Five Elements. And that something is my system for
learning. Now I have a learning system that centers around
books, note-taking, teaching and talks. This was in no way
planned, and it may or may not evolve further. All I know is
that my life is devoted to learning and teaching. The bulk of
my learning comes from reading books. Second to that is
learning by way of listening to podcasts, conducting interviews, watching movies (mostly documentaries) and asking
questions. The books, interviews, note-taking and teaching
are systematic. They follow the same format day to day, week
to week. Speaking events are as frequent as the market demands, and the documentaries and podcasts come as time /
situations permit. Learning is as much a part of my life as
training and exercise. It is a part of my fabric.

My podcast schedule became my new system

This book has let me share how a teacher-turned-professional-fighter became a teacher again. AMX has taken on a life of its own, which is one of the coolest things that can happen. "Google" means something both as a noun and a verb (even if Google does steer you away from the verb use). "Uber" means something. "Nike" stands for something. My drive is a fascination with creating something of my own. Innovation is used in business to evolve and improve. As individuals, we are all told we can do anything we want, but then we are told by those same people what can and can't work. We're caught in this total mindfudge: An encouragement of absolute self-belief set forth in us from a young age pitted against a set of limitations and guidelines in which we are supposed to work. Guess what? I don't like a lot of the business guidelines being set forth by experts. I simply don't align with them. They don't ring true to me. I don't think life and business can be boiled down into a tagline or value prop. I don't enjoy sales funnels and upsells as a consumer, so I don't want to use them as the seller. In what could potentially be seen as arrogance, I don't think 99% of business people "get it" at all (this coming from a guy who is yet to capture any real sort of success in business). I think they've simply discovered a way to package a product and sell it. Accruing social media and followers and becoming a best-selling author is sadly not about being an interesting person and writing an incredibly interesting book, it's about influencing the system or heck, even buying stinking followers!

AMX is me, pure and simple. It is a noun in that it is a show, AM Excellence. It's also a verb that means to learn, study, explore, connect, teach and entertain. What exactly am I teaching? Life. I'm hellbent on making the most out of my existence, and I'm calling on the wisdom and experience of others to help me best achieve that end. In time, with enough practice and repetition, certain ideas and philosophies will stick, and others will fade away. Eventually, the sticky ones will make up me, my truth. AMX is my systematic approach to learning so that I can breathe peacefully to my last moment on Earth, and there's no reason to keep that all to myself. Lesson planning, taking notes and producing shows is my way of synthesizing and making sense of my learnings.

"Why learn?" you may be asking yourself. Learning gets you what you want. Learning is the key ingredient to life. It is a part of Natural Law. From the very beginning, it was key to our survival. Where does food come from? How do we cultivate fields? How do we create fire? What are the best ways to hunt? Build a house? Survive? Thrive? One of my favorite parts of watching my kids grow is watching them learn and discover. Learning allows us to get to our honest selves. AMX'ing has become one of my most important practices.

What happens after a lifetime of reading is, you kind of become your own book. All this information goes into your brain. Some of it's going to go right out the other side of your brain. Some of it you're going to retain in moments that you least expect it. Then eventually you become the books that you read.
AMXtalks 94

(This was my commenting on the book) There is power in learning. It helps you communicate better, giving you points of references, general facts to include in conversation, as well as overall confidence in your ability to communicate effectively.
Ted Turner
Call Me Ted
AMXbooks 302

When I decided "I'm gonna change my life," then I said, "I'm gonna pursue this martial arts, this fighting thing with every ounce of my soul." I pursued every aspect of it—that included going to the gym and learning the techniques, and that included reading every single book that I could.
Matt "The Immortal" Brown
UFC Fighter
AMXtalks 185

Curiosity has, quite literally, been the key to my success, and also the key to my happiness.
Brian Grazer
A Curious Mind
AMXbooks 497

A lot of people are mentally fat, mentally overweight. You need to get in shape. Build a six-pack of your mind. You need to be shredded.
Niyi Sobo
CEO & Peak Mindset Consultant / NFL Veteran
AMXtalks 153

I've mentioned it before, but my wife has said to me a number of times, "It's most difficult to be your wife during your transitions." She's referring to transitioning from teaching to the UFC and from the UFC to post-UFC. There's always a period of time during transitions where you are totally unsure about where to go and which decisions to make, and you're totally stressed at your unsureness. One of the best ways I've heard it put is in the Vince Lombardi biography *When Pride Still Mattered*. Because of his constant stress and anxiety, his circle would refer to him as "Mr. High-Low". It's extremely difficult to stay balanced when pursuing something great, so rest easy knowing that it happens to the best of the best. Needless to say, post-fighting, I was stuck. I didn't know where to go, and I was (still am) Mr. High-Low. I needed to devise a way, close to home and cost efficient (no fights = no income) that enabled me to thrive on my association with "the best."

BOOKS! Aha! I would read more and more books! I would satiate my desire to spend every day with the world's most intelligent, successful, hard-working and influential people by spending more of my time reading.

CONVERSATIONS! Aha! I would intentionally set up and initiate conversations with the same types of people I read about and spent 25 years of my life competing with / against.

And thus was born was *A Fighter's Mindset* (later SPANIARD101, and now *The Spaniard Show*) and eventually, AM Excellence (AMX).

When you're around the world's best on a daily basis, as I was fighting, you are pulled to a higher level of being. Your environment influences the way you think and, accordingly, the way you act. You can actually transform yourself by transforming your surroundings. I became a world-class fighter by being around world-class fighters and doing what world-class fighters did.

I had always been a reader and questioner, but post-fighting, I began a more systematic approach to learning. I would spend more time reading, take copious notes from my learnings and extract how the lessons fit into my life. I would seek out and converse with people from whom I wanted to learn. I took a very active approach because I needed a way to make up for the lack of purpose and discipline that I no longer had. I needed to create my own world of "the best."

It's almost as if the process became the game. There was

no opponent staring me in the face or looming over me for months. Instead, there was every day, every morning and the urge to never settle for mediocrity. I'm not superhuman—I need mental fuel to operate at such a high level, and books and conversations are that fuel. Couple that mental fuel with a consistent fitness routine, and you'll be one high-octane-operating-son-of-a-gun!

We have the privilege and opportunity to study and learn from the greats. There is no fast-tracking experience and you can't know what you don't know, but you CAN know what they know, simply by studying and understanding what worked and what didn't. As Jack Canfield says (Success Principle #9) "Success Leaves Clues." And I'm following them all the way.

19

**THE END
of the Beginning**

Why I want you to take BOTH my titles

This is and is not the end of the book. It's not the end of the book, because more pages come after this chapter, and within those pages are more of what I've been talking about: LEARNING.

But it is the end of the book, sorta, for a couple reasons. The final part of this chapter was previously the end of the book, but something wasn't sitting right with Dread. He didn't feel like the ending did justice to the book where it was, so we shuffled it forward.

That is one example of how a book comes together, or at least how this one did. I sincerely hope that one day I get to talk you through the nuts and bolts of it. It's mind-blowing.

The other way that this chapter is the end of the book is that it sums up what I want to tell you and hopefully inspire you to do ... BECOME a lifelong learner. That means learning and applying what you're learning. You will be DOING

LEARNING, the act of it. It'll help you become a better you.

I recently finished the book *The Happiness Hypothesis*, and it included the Greek term *arête*, defined as excellence or virtue, especially of a functional or purposeful kind. It also has to do with living to one's full potential. A great example in *The Happiness Hypothesis* is that the *arête* of a knife is to cut well. This led me to think that the *arête* of a fighter is to fight well. It's cool to talk about fighting, wear fight t-shirts and possibly even train to fight, but fighters actually have to fight, and fight regularly.

How does that relate to being the World's Toughest Lifelong Learner? To my mission of embodying and inspiring lifelong learning? Well, I wouldn't very much embody and inspire lifelong learning if I didn't actually DO that, and do it regularly. I wouldn't very much be the World's Toughest Lifelong Learner if I wasn't tough and wasn't continually learning. The *arête* of the WTLL is to train physically and mentally, and to do it day after day.

I want so very much for you to buy into this idea of lifelong learning. Not because I get something from it, rather because YOU will get something from it. Two days ago—and you'll especially appreciate this if you're married—my wife actually said to her best friend, "Charlie reads a lot of self-help books, and it's definitely helping our relationship." "YES!" I said to myself. Through a committed practice of lifelong learning, you will become more empathetic, well-spoken and valuable, in the sense that you will know more and know how to do more. You will have more hope, belief in yourself and "I'm OK"-ness because you'll learn what others have experienced and how they got through their problems and challenges, and you'll see that you can do the same. You'll smile more because many books are funny. You'll create a piece of every day—your learning time—that you look forward to because you know it will help you in every area of your life. You will have a positive association with learning and goodness.

I have become the World's Toughest Lifelong Learner because I set aside the time to MAKE myself the World's Toughest Lifelong Learner and RE-make myself the World's Toughest Lifelong Learner every day. Lifelong learning doesn't end until, well, life ends. Makes sense, right? It's like showering and training—if you don't want to stink and get weaker, you do it every day. I say that as a joke, but you get the point. Every day and every conversation is an opportunity to learn.

Way back in the beginning of this book, I said this:

If you're looking to understand how an unspecial kid from small-town Hollidaysburg, Pennsylvania, became the WORLD'S TOUGHEST LIFELONG LEARNER, and how you can use all of those tools and experiences in your own way, to write your own story, to create your own thing—good! Too often we sit back and wait for them to do the thing, for them to win the title, for them to go to the place. They have what it takes, and I don't. Bollocks to that! As I'm proclaiming my WTLL title, I'm also issuing a friendly challenge, or rather, a call to a shared experience. Why should I, The Spaniard, hold the title World's Toughest Lifelong Learner? Why shouldn't you? Why is this never-ending quest for knowledge, and the spoils that go along with it, reserved for me, and not you? Answer: It's not. Grab that stinkin' seat belt and strap in. We're going for a ride!

It's been a long journey together through these pages, but your real journey is just getting started. The ride is over, please exit right. Your feet are now on the ground, and you are well-equipped with the tools and know-how to become your own version of the World's Toughest Lifelong Learner. I firmly believe that the best life you can live is one with life-long learning at the front and center of your noggin. You were meant to learn and grow. For real. Like actually. Our whole purpose is to learn and grow and repeat the process. IT IS LIFE'S CYCLE, for crying out loud! All each of us did at the beginning of life was learn ... that is, until we forgot about learning, because we thought we'd learned enough. But we haven't. I haven't. You haven't. Now we're bringing learning back!

My message to Gracie and Rocky: As your father (re-member, Reader, I'm talking to Gracie and Rocky; I'm not ac-tually *your* father), I think it would be cool if you grew up to love training and sports and competition and wrestling, but it's not really what I want. What I actually want is for you to embrace a life of learning and allow it to take you wherever it takes you, as long as you give all of yourself and are kind to people along the way. I want you to ask questions and follow your curiosity because I believe that's what life is about. I be-lieve it's a big part of what makes us happy, and I want you to be happy. It's how I am discovering myself, even at 38 years old, and I believe it's how you will discover yourself ... and the world ... and other people. Life is a gift, and learning will help you receive and use that gift.

I don't want you to be me. I want you to be you. I just want to set an example of someone who tries their best, is kind to other people and who embraces lifelong learning. There are many mountains to climb in life, and they'll never go away. Whenever you reach the base of a mountain, I want you to remember that learning is the way up. What you want is up there, and learning gets you what you want. Learning is your foundation. It's that seemingly empty space between where you are and where you want to go. That void is not really a void. It's simply an unoccupied space that is waiting to be filled with time and effort. And if you fill that seemingly empty space with time and effort, in the end you'll win. You'll win because you tried, and you learned. That's life.

I want you to be a Spaniard. It stands for any bold explorer.

I'm working on leaving a giant dent in the earth. A giant imprint on the universe. When I say "Spaniard," I don't mean me, Charlie, or even my fight name. When I say "Spaniard," I mean the idea, the vision that I have for Spaniard that will still be here when I'm long dead and gone, when the world is passing by, generations from now. I'm not focused on Charlie, I'm focused on what Spaniard represents. I want Spaniard to be something that changes the world.

Dread and I are in the nascent stages. Our goal is big, it's ginormous. It's daunting, it's scary, it's intimidating. It's laughable to some people. It may be roll-your-eyes-able to some people. But the truth is, I don't care, because I believe it, and I believe in it.

At the end of the day, I'm a dude who reads books and talks about them. I'm a guy with an insatiable thirst for knowledge. I have a curiosity that I see in my kids, and though frustrating at times (as my curiosity can be to others), it brings joy to my heart. My truest self is bringing my curiosity and love of learning to light. It's how I make sense of the world and my own experiences. And I believe it's my best chance of bringing good to the world. I'm writing this book and continuing my journey because I want to help you figure out your best chance of bringing good to the world.

I am The Spaniard. I want you to be The Spaniard. I am The World's Toughest Lifelong Learner. I want you to be the The World's Toughest Lifelong Learner. Because life is hard, and you have to fight. But the fight is glorious.

So let's make the most of this time in the cage. There's the bell now. Let's GO.

> *(This was my commenting on the book) If every day is a fight, then Every Day is your opponent, and he's coming for you every day.*
> **Ted Turner**
> **Call Me Ted**
> *AMXbooks 306*

> *I want to fight you, Day! And I ain't goin' anywhere.*
> *AMXtalks 170*

Extras

One of the challenges of writing this book was organizing and including everything we wanted without taking it too far. I have journals, show notes—all kinds of documents filled with inspiring, insightful, educational and entertaining content—but the unfortunate fact is that we can't include it all. After some thought exploration and dead-ends, Dread and I came up with what is the rest of the book. We came to think of the following pieces of writing as articles, because they can stand alone, but you'll see the similarity to earlier chapters. Just like deleted scenes on a DVD (I say this knowing that we are in the final days of DVDs), they could very well have appeared in the main feature, but they just didn't seem to work in the flow.

It's fitting for my second memoir to end with an Extras section, because my first memoir, *DRIVEN*, did as well. Here are the three articles:

Deep Dives: 3 Topics That Changed How I Think

Accountability Matters Even More Than I Thought

Figuring Out My Identity

Deep Dives: 3 Topics That Changed How I Think

I often read books / have conversations that challenge me, make me uncomfortable or even throw me into anxiety. It's like you've lived life a certain way and all of a sudden you hit a ginormous wall—there's a big elephant in the room. Things don't make sense any more because they conflict with what I thought before or what a lot of other people think. It's especially tough when those other people are family and friends. Or the new info might conflict with pleasant nostalgia that I feel from reflecting on the past, like when you learn that things weren't what they seemed back in the day.

These ideas put a new light on things that were securely fastened in my life paradigm. I'm forced to examine my own thoughts and beliefs. That's stinkin' scary. The certainty that you thought you had might not exist anymore.

The upside of receiving this information is that it becomes a new part of your world. It makes things more understandable and familiar. I think that's what empathy is about—fewer things seem crazy or weird or totally wrong.

That's what learning does—it expands your world by bringing in new things, and many of these things can be helpful. It makes you more well rounded and well-equipped to deal with life's situations. In a sense, you're doing your homework. To bring in a good ol' Spanish example, learning is about developing the *cojones* to go to unfamiliar places, and—wait a minute, weren't the conquistadors Spanish??? It's all coming together!

Along with this new learning comes the reality that you've got to make sense of it. You have to work through the discrepancies that exist between what you thought, what you learned, and what you think now. And you'll also see that there's not always a black / white / yes / no answer. You might say to yourself, "There are some open loops that now exist in my beliefs, and I'm okay with that. Things won't always make sense. I've been forced to loosen my need for control."

You'll also find yourself internally debating whether or not here-and-now is the time to bring up the new information you've learned. Maybe it'll make someone think differently of you. Maybe you'll start an argument or debate.

I'm still learning to do all of this. I'm working through it, as will you. Wrestling and fighting are sports and lifestyles that I've dedicated myself to, but they also represent two words often used when facing life's challenges: "We'll fight through it ... I'm wrestling with what I should do." My chosen sports have prepared me well for life. Symbolically, books and learning will do the same for you.

I often text Dread things like:

> *What do I do with this information that conflicts with other things I have always thought?*

Or with information that is different from the info that those around me have?

And he and I talk through it. All I can say is that I don't have a final answer. Life is fluid. I'm trying my best, and that's all I can do. Same goes for you, right?

Here are some quotes that illustrate what I'm saying:

One of the most important ways I use curiosity every day is to see the world through other people's eyes.
Brian Grazer
A Curious Mind
AMXbooks 498

The more I know about the world, the more I understand about how the world works, the more people I know, the more perspectives I have—the more likely it is that I'll have a good idea.
Brian Grazer
A Curious Mind
AMXbooks 502

The power of committing yourself to learning is: You hear all these different ideas, and there's a lot of different ways to do the right thing, and it forces you to really articulate in your own heart and mind what you believe.
AMXtalks 181

Here are topics that I found extra-perspective-shaping:

Native American history

Anybody that thinks that the government is inherently good for people needs to take a close look at the ex-

perience of Native Americans on reservations, be-
cause it wasn't an easy time.
Brett Chapman
Native American Advocate / Attorney
AMXtalks 197

Americans who have always looked westward when
reading about this period should read this book facing
eastward.
Dee Brown
Bury My Heart at Wounded Knee
AMXbooks 546

The Sand Creek Massacre is something I believe we
should all know about. It's not easy to read about, but
it happened, and it's part of our history.
Dee Brown
Bury My Heart at Wounded Knee
AMXbooks 549

Some quotes regarding the destruction of the North
American buffalo (to help eradicate the Native Ameri-
cans): "Let them kill, skin and sell until the buffalo is
exterminated, as it is the only way to bring lasting
peace and allow civilization to advance" (General
Sheridan) ... "endless desolation of bones and skulls
and rotting hooves" ... "thunder of a million hooves
would have shaken the prairie" (a few years earlier)
Dee Brown
Bury My Heart at Wounded Knee
AMXbooks 553

I'm extremely grateful to have developed an interest in
Native American history and culture later in life. From spiri-
tuality and connectedness to the Earth, to the political and
cultural aspects of the development of the U.S., Native Amer-

icans have a rich and complex history in our (their) country. Just as young German children are required to learn a great deal about the Holocaust so that it doesn't happen again, I feel like learning about Native Americans should be treated as a central part in our youth's history curriculum. Everything I've studied has opened my eyes to the reality that a dark spot looms in our history.

Plant medicines

The one thing that has taught me the most in life, without question, is plant medicines. In the right context, done appropriately, with respect and reverence, and with intention.
Kyle Kingsbury
Former UFC Fighter / Host, Kyle Kingsbury Podcast
AMXtalks 189

Prior to being exposed to the world of plant medicines and psychedelics by way of Kyle Kingsbury and Aubrey Marcus, I would've thought it was crazy, they were crazy, and it made no sense. But then I met them and talked to them and learned about their beliefs and values. Especially with Kyle, someone with whom I had grown close over the years, I had to look at all of this new knowledge with a clear lens. I could not discount the fact that he's a mentor of mine, very well studied, super intelligent and an overall great person. That whether or not I agreed or disagreed was almost irrelevant. I was in it for the learning and teaching. I was fascinated, so much so that I bought and read Michael Pollan's *How to Change Your Mind* (I'm finishing it up on AMXbooks the day after I write this). I look back at this whole area of knowledge with reverence. I would never have thought that I'd know and appreciate so much about psychedelics. I'm not signing up to go on a Vision Quest in South America, but I'm not NOT signing up, either. I'm just on this learning wave loving every minute of it.

Astrophysics

Did you know that the Big Bang happened 13.8 billion years ago? And because of it, our universe went from "one-trillionth the size of the period that ends this sentence" to what it is today (46 billion light years and expanding). P.S. Dinosaurs only became extinct 65 million years ago. That's less than 2% of the Earth's past!
Neil deGrasse Tyson
Astrophysics for People in a Hurry
AMXbooks 579

Earth, as a cosmic object, is remarkably smooth. If you had a super-duper, jumbo-gigantic finger, and you dragged it against Earth's surface (oceans and all), Earth would feel as smooth as a cue ball.
Neil deGrasse Tyson
Astrophysics for People in a Hurry
AMXbooks 580

I want to make a special point of acknowledging that this book on astrophysics was one time when I faced the fundamental uncomfortability that learning this content and believing it might conflict with my Catholic background. That's what learning does. It can be scary. It forces you to think through things. If a topic scares you, head right into it, just like a buffalo plods straight into a storm (something I learned from Chad Miller in AMXtalks 110)—to get through the hard part and find the calm.

Accountability Matters
Even More Than I Thought

Success Principle #1 - Take 100% Responsibility for Your Life
Jack Canfield
The Success Principles
AMXbooks 422

The leader must own everything in his or her world. There is no one else to blame.
Jocko Willink / Leif Babin
Extreme Ownership
AMXbooks 467

I think I take losses better than wins, because in my mind, I've never lost because someone was better than me. It was my fault. I get what I earn.
Spencer Lee
World-Class Wrestling Champion
AMXtalks 87

One thing after another derailed his plan to go to Greece: Kids, work, mortgage. Or were these just excuses?
Dean Karnazes
The Road to Sparta
AMXbooks 287

Next year is always a year away.
Russ Roberts
How Adam Smith Can Change Your Life
AMXbooks 396

I already had a sense of the importance of Accountability. It's one of the Five Elements. But it stands out among
what I've learned during this part of my journey and de-
serves extra emphasis. Accountability is a word no one wants
to hear, acknowledge or come to grips with. But it's crucial for
you to understand that no one is coming to save you.

I've always understood the premise of accountability.
My parents made it very clear that the decisions we make
have consequences, good and bad. That shaped the way I operated when I was young and still operate today, and as I get
older and wiser, I'm learning that there are levels upon levels
of accountability. There's the once-in-a-while type, the casual
type, the genuinely-aware-and-well-intended type and then
my type—the kind who thought they were as accountable as
they come until they read the aforementioned book *Extreme
Ownership.* Having read the book, I can't get into a single argument with my wife without hearing an echo in my mind
of "Extreme ownership, Charlie ... Extreme ownership, Charlie ... Extreme ownership." The idea of Extreme Ownership is
exactly what it sounds like. There are no tricks or fancy steps
in the process. You stop dishing blame or excuses outward
before they even start. One idea I took from the book and use
in my talks is: Don't blame, complain or make excuses. Try it
out for a day. The next time you're about to do one of these
three non-Extreme-Ownership actions, stop and repeat the
mantra, "Don't blame, complain or make excuses."

As I sit here writing this book, alone in my house, fully believing that I have what it takes to be the best in the world, yet widely unrecognized for writing and speaking, I grow frustrated. "Why? Why? Why?" I ask myself. "I know I'm as good as the rest of them, so why is it taking so long to achieve success?" I wallow for a bit, but then I remember that the only person who is going to get me where I want to go is ME, and it's won't happen by sitting here doing nothing. I need to stay centered and do what needs to be done.

As a professional fighter, I was scared to death. It's terrifying getting into a locked cage to fight another man, someone trained to dominate you and 100% focused on that. As fighters, we have months to think about the fight. It's the last thing on your mind before you fall asleep and the first thing upon waking up. It really is terrifying and unsettling, but living with that constant fear and uncomfortability caused a switch to go off inside of me. I realized—really, really realized—that it was all on me. Yes, I'd have a team that would help me prepare and a supporting cast of friends, family and fans for moral support, but at the end of the day, there were two people entering that cage: Me and the guy who wanted to destroy me. That, my friends, is accountability.

Enforcing in pro hockey

The guy who disrespects people and disrespects situations, then all of a sudden gets smoked in the mouth —that's just karma. That should happen more often. Fear is a powerful thing. Accountability is a powerful thing. That's how respect is generated and bred.
Riley Cote
Cannabis / Hemp Activist / Former NHL Enforcer
AMXtalks 137

One of the most fascinating conversations I've had since starting my show was with Riley Cote, former NHL enforcer with the Philadelphia Flyers, and it pertains big-time to accountability. An enforcer in the NHL is the guy who fights the opponents who get out of line. I'd always been aware of the term, and as a less-than-casual hockey fan, I thought I had a general understanding of what the position was and why it existed. But spending an hour talking with Riley opened my eyes to the themes and principles that existed beneath the surface when it came to his position. We were two peas in a pod connected by our love and respect for fighting.

On how fighting can create a sense of order and peace, Riley said, "There's something to be said about getting punched in the face and having some sense punched into you. You can learn a lot by getting your a** beat. Especially if you get your a** beat for the right reasons." I'm writing this knowing full well that some of you will disagree with Riley's logic, but as a professional fighter, I am 100% in line with his rationale. While the world has changed such that it's not always as simple as it used to be, take what Riley says and fully digest it before discarding it. For those of you who "get it," you'll find yourself nodding in agreement with his wisdom.

I'm not suggesting that you sign up for the next professional fight in your town, but what if you operated with A Fighter's Mindset? What if you prepared for every day as if you were about to enter a cage and settle things the old-fashioned way? What if you prepared to face every bit of fear, adversity, negativity, resistance and challenge like a professional fighter preparing for a fight? What if you lived out the ideals of Rocky? A professional fighter knows what's coming his way. He embraces the challenge. He prepares for it with all of his being. He believes that he will win but is well aware of the risks and unpredictability of what he's about to do. There is no other way. He attacks it *mano a mano*.

My whole business model is based on a paradoxical concept. I have this thing that I know people need (learning), but they don't know they need it. And the only way they'll know they need it is to consume it, but they don't feel overly compelled to consume it because they don't know its value. So how the heck will it happen? Well, I need to make it happen. I need to demonstrate to them the extreme value of consistently and repeatedly engaging in high-level learning and conversation. In the third year, after over 1000 episodes and dozens of presentations, I'm finally starting to make a dent.

In his book *The War of Art*, Steven Pressfield wrote, "Nothing is as empowering as real-world validation, even if it's failure." That is exactly why I love wrestling and fighting so much. It puts you right in front of everything. There is no place to hide. There were eight men who were simply better than I was on fight night throughout my 27-fight career. That's real-world validation. What am I going to do about it?

Unfortunately, in today's world, accountability is going by the wayside. Social media and a general sense of entitlement have thrown this age-old principle out the window. True, we can't go around fighting everybody—that's just not how the world operates—but we can commit to living with accountability. We can commit to owning our words and actions and being fully aware that they bring consequences.

I've learned, as much as anything, that people respect hard work. The more you put your head down, keep your nose to the grindstone, embrace hard work and challenge, the more likely it is that someone, somewhere will come along and help you. People who work hard or have created something special in life know the work it takes to do something special and want to reward other young people who are following that same path. I wouldn't hold your breath for that person to appear, but know that it does happen.

Make a decision to not let your environment become an excuse. My buddy Dave didn't. While his parents are supportive and loving, they are recovering alcoholics and were unable to provide the home life stability that would be considered normal or expected. At one point in college, he was in control of his family's finances, with the debit card in hand. This was at a time when my parents were still paying for nearly everything I did. I was amazed at Dave's maturity and ease of operating at such a responsible level. We were in college. We were supposed to be free of major worry and responsibility outside of exams and sports. His responsibility and actions stemmed from years of practice. He had assumed this role at one point in junior / senior high by deciding he would make the best of his situation.

Another great example of not letting your surroundings dictate where you go in life is The Rock. As you have heard, he is one of the people I aspire to emulate when it comes to hard work. Though we know him from professional wrestling, movies, television and social media, it was not always that way. At one point, in 1995, after having been cut from the Canadian Football League, The Rock had $7 to his name (hence the name of his production company, Seven Bucks Production). But look at him now.

Keep. On. Fighting!

I get a lot of inquiries about helping people in one way or another: How to become a professional fighter, start an exercise program, lose weight, write a book, start a podcast. And it makes me feel extremely good and helpful to do what I can. But I've been contacted enough times to know that the vast majority of people are never going to make a change. A buffer of "Contact me next week" (or some other simple but telling task) is an effective first step to sift the "doers" from the "not-doers".

There have been cases when the person doesn't follow through, and I feel it like a gut punch. That's when it's a friend who needs help. But I have to let it go. It's not up to me to convince anyone. You have to learn it for yourself. If you reach out but then fade away, there's nothing I can do. You have to be ready to change. One of Jim Rohn's famous sayings is, "You can't hire someone else to do your push-ups for you." I once heard Cael Sanderson (undefeated, 4-time NCAA Champion / Olympic gold medalist / Penn State University Wrestling Coach) speak at a wrestling event. When asked how he is able to get his guys to do such and such, he responded in a very calm, humble manner, stating that he can only do so much. Paraphrased, he said: "At the end of the day, it's on the guys." At the end of the day, it's on you.

How Derek made himself a champ

In the spring of 2016, I received an email from Bob, a dedicated grandfather, regarding his grandson, Derek. Through mutual friends in New Hampshire, Bob had heard of me and what I was doing and was interested in setting up an in-person mind / body session for his grandson. Derek had been a lifelong wrestler, and entering his senior year he had not reached the success he so much yearned for. As part of his graduation gift, Bob and I arranged an afternoon of intensity for Derek.

This was tied to my philosophy of consistently pushing your mind and body and the benefit of doing so. The recipe is simple: Push your physical self to your breaking point, and then a little bit further. Then regroup and talk it out. I'm not reinventing the wheel here, either. Military training is based on breaking soldiers down to build them back up. My session with Derek was designed to do the exact same thing.

In July 2016, Derek and Bob made their way to PA for an experience that would leave a lasting imprint on all three of us. Derek and I trained side by side, exhausting our physical and mental selves. Derek's words (AMXtalks 66): "After two sets, I was still shaking, and you were still motivating me, saying, 'You gotta keep pushing it.'" Derek said my words would stick with him forever: "Whatever you're doing, re-member why you're there." Derek was spent. I was spent. Af-ter cleaning up, we sat down and talked over lunch. That's it. We talked, but there's something to be said for talking IF it's backed up by hard work. In his book *On the Air!*, Napoleon Hill states, "Astounding things can happen when two or more people get together and continuously meet and discuss the things they want to do." This ties into Hill's mastermind group principle (as defined earlier in the book), "an alliance of two or more people working in harmony, perfect harmony, with a positive mental attitude for the attainment of a defi-nite end." Though Derek and I didn't technically have a mas-termind, in one powerful afternoon, by establishing and talk-ing through his goals, coupled with a grueling training ses-sion, Derek left with one thing on his mind: State title.

Derek's podcast episode and story is a great example of John Wooden's "Product vs. Byproduct" concept. The product is what you control. It's the day-to-day work and thousands of tiny decisions that go into accomplishing anything great.

The byproduct is the result. In our episode, I said, "The byproduct is the medal, the wrestling, the things, the goals. The product is what you control, and that's exactly what you just said: You control your work, you control your mindset, you control the type of person you are, you control the type of people you surround yourself with. You control the daily decisions and choices and habits that you live by."

Derek and Bob made their way back to New Hampshire, and Derek and I maintained contact via social media. It was several months until I heard from Bob again. On February 21, 2017, I received an email that brought me to tears:

> As you are aware, we had an incredible Saturday. Derek won the D-I State Championship at 138 lbs. It was an unbelievable effort and the culmination of many hours of training and hard work on his part. The seeds of that intensity were sown from his time spent with you in August. He came away from that experience with a sense of purpose and focus that drove him to the success that he received Saturday night. You were the agent of change that made it possible for him to believe that he could achieve his goal.
>
> Derek trained twice a day at least three or four times a week, taking off only one day each week. He placed mats in his bedroom on the floor and around the walls so he could work on drills, he set up an area in his basement to work on footwork drills, he joined a private wrestling club, which he has done each fall, to get ready for the season, he did most of his road work wearing an elevation mask to increase his cardio, he consistently used his chin-up bar in his bedroom doorway and cranked out hundreds of pushups six days a week, he had a regular grip strengthening routine that he did religiously, he joined a gym to be able

to vary his workouts, he wrote down his goals and looked at them every day—and more. He did all this so he would have no regrets about not being prepared.

Derek's success is a great story and embodies a great many of the things that I teach to audiences. I'm grateful to have had even a small part in providing Derek with a truly transformational experience that will serve him well as he goes to college and beyond.

On the episode about Derek, Dread stressed that Derek illustrated that inevitably you have to DO IT. "You could talk to him about the mindset and exercises that would help, but between his experiences with you and the championship is: He has to do it. He has to make that decision and work when he doesn't feel like it." The letter describes a training montage straight out of a Rocky movie. What I replied to Dread was:

I interact with a lot of people. Most of those times, I'm in, then I talk-inspire-leave. I always emphasize when I leave: I'm not going to see you tomorrow or the next day or the next day. I put out content for you to keep that message alive in your heart, but you have to do it. I can't do it. I can't come to your school. I can't follow you home. Derek didn't look to me, look to his grandfather, look to anyone else to get it done. He got it done.
AMXtalks 65

The Iron Law of You states that you think more about yourself than you think of me. The Iron Law of Me states that I think more about myself than I do about you.
Russ Roberts
How Adam Smith Can Change Your Life
AMXbooks 394

"You're the only person that's gonna fight for you. I don't care if you have an agent or whoever. The biggest advocate for you is you. I don't care if you're an accountant or you pump gas, you're in charge of whatever it is you want to become."
Cowboy Gator Magraw (Mike Kinney)
Professional Wrestler
AMXtalks 136

(After a bad dealing with a distributor) The experience taught Ben & Jerry that no one else was going to make the same commitment to their product that they did. Ben & Jerry's was their life.
Fred "Chico" Lager
Ben & Jerry's: The Inside Scoop
AMXbooks 376

To close out these thoughts on accountability, consider this: Drew Manning (AMXtalks 118) of fit2fat2fit.com (go there, his story will blow your mind) said, "You can't pour from an empty cup. If you don't take care of yourself first, you can't give to other relationships." Simple and powerful. Take care of yourself, and impact those around you.

Figuring Out My Identity

Keeping life open-ended makes it exciting. Things come and go. Life changes. As I got older and came to realize that more and more, I had a lot to learn about identity. It's still a bit confusing, to be honest. My values are stable, but even they change. The ability to stay grounded while also being open to change is tricky. I'm in the early stages of figuring it out, but it'll happen.

Jim Carrey lays it out well in the Netflix documentary *Jim and Andy: The Great Beyond*:

> I'd lay on my bed, and I'd think, "What do they want? What do they want? What do they want?" It wasn't what I wanted. I knew what I wanted: I wanted to be successful, I wanted to be a famous actor. But what do THEY want? What do THEY want? What do THEY want? And then one day in the middle of the night, I woke up out of a sound sleep and sat up in bed and went, "They want to be free from concern." And the light bulb went off: They need to be free from concern, so I'm gonna be the guy who's free from concern.
> **Jim Carrey**
> **Jim and Andy: The Great Beyond**

I think a LOT about entertainers—comedians, actors and musicians, in particular. My interviews have included many entertainers:

(These are all AMXtalks episodes)

77	Max Major, World-Renowned Mentalist
120	Kye Smith, Drummer & YouTube Star
171	Gabriel The Gun, "No Doubt" Musician & Motivational Gangster
176	Richard Turner, Card Mechanic
186	Laurie Berkner, Master of Kids' Music
193	Jamie Kilstein, Comedian / Podcaster with Jiu Jitsu Roots

I've studied books by entertainment stars:

Steve Martin	*Born Standing Up*
Brian Grazer	*A Curious Mind*
Kevin Hart	*I Can't Make This Up*
Trevor Noah	*Born a Crime*

Entertainers make people feel something. In their souls. At their core. That is powerful, and that is exactly what I want to do. I want to remind you that you're human and you feel. At the end of the day, I want to make you feel happy, and my conduit to doing so is by way of my own learning and curiosity. Mister Rogers' mentor, Dr. Margaret McFarland, once instructed an artist visiting her students to simply "love clay in front of them". They would absorb the lesson. That idea has helped guide me: I simply want to "love learning" in front of you. She goes on to say that "attitudes aren't taught, they're caught." May you catch my energy of loving learning, and may it make you feel happy.

Life is a story. It's full of chapters. And the beauty of life is that not only do you get to choose how you interpret each chapter, but your interpretation writes the next chapter ... So why not choose the one that serves your life best?
Kevin Hart
I Can't Make this Up
AMXbooks 556

(Quote from Eddie Murphy) My advice is don't ask for advice ... trust yourself and your own way of doing things. Just because something worked for someone else doesn't mean it's gonna work for you.
Kevin Hart
I Can't Make this Up
AMXbooks 566

Rule #8 - Tell the Truth or At Least Don't Lie
You are by no means only what you already know. You are also all that which you could know, if only you would.
Jordan Peterson
12 Rules for Life
AMXbooks 462

Self-awareness (Principle 1) can lead you to finding your True North, and that will make all the difference.
Joe De Sena
The Spartan Way
AMXbooks 572

My job is to ask questions. I'm not sure I could have a better job ever. It's like getting paid to sleep, for someone who likes sleeping.
AMXtalks 73

Guests Featured on *The Spaniard Show*
As of this book's publication

GUEST	Arts/Entertainment/Writing	Business/Career	History/Nation/Law	Life/Family	Media/Technology	Military/Veterans	Outdoors/Adventure	Spirituality/Philosophy	Performance/Effectiveness	Science/Nature	Sports	Health/Wellness/Training
Adam Chubb, Well-Traveled Pro Basketball Player											x	
Adam Hluschak, Former Wrestler Still Training at Level 10				x							x	
Adee Cazayoux, Athlete, Nutrition Guru, Renaissance Woman												x
Amanda Rondon Team RWB & Old Glory Relay			x			x						
Amelia Boone, Pro Athlete & Attorney, Both Full-Time!							x					
Andrea Waltz, "Go For No" Co-Author & Sales Trainer		x										
Andy Dziedzic, Illegal Dishwasher Turned Financial Pro		x										
Andy Main, MMA Champ and Rational Ronin											x	
Ángel Sanz, Pro Basketball Veteran & ACTUAL Spaniard			x								x	

GUEST	Arts/Entertainment/Writing	Business/Career	History/Nation/Law	Life/Family	Media/Technology	Military/Veterans	Outdoors/Adventure	Spirituality/Philosophy	Performance/Effectiveness	Science/Nature	Sports	Health/Wellness/Training
Ariel Helwani, World's Leading MMA Journalist				x	x						x	
Ashleigh Williamson, Rebuilder of Her Own Life				x								
Barry Krammes, World-Class in Javelin											x	
Ben "ChAD" Brenneman				x							x	
Ben Askren, Wrestler/MMA Champ, In That Order											x	
Betsy Padamonsky, Broadway Performer	x											
Bill Simpson, Retired President & CEO, Hershey Entertainment & Resorts		x		x								
Brandon Steiner, Resilient Founder of Steiner Sports		x									x	
Brett Chapman, Native American Attorney with "Wounded Knee" Ties			x									
Brian Dickinson, Navy Rescue Swimmer, Mountaineer, Author of *Blind Descent*						x	x					
Brian Jennings, NFL Player, Brain Health Optimizer											x	x

GUEST	Arts/Entertainment/Writing	Business/Career	History/Nation/Law	Life/Family	Media/Technology	Military/Veterans	Outdoors/Adventure	Spirituality/Philosophy	Performance/Effectiveness	Science/Nature	Sports	Health/Wellness/Training
Chad Miller, Thriving after Surviving the Storms of Life				X								
Chael Sonnen, MMA Fighter & Broadcaster					X						X	
Charlie Elison of the Travis Manion Foundation						X						
Charlie Engle, Record-Setting Ultrarunner & Adventurer							X					
Chef Jonny Mac of Rival Bros. Coffee Roasters		X		X								
Chris "CROM" Romulo, Muay Thai Fighter/Trainer											X	
Chris Mocko, Techie Turned Ultrarunning YouTuber					X		X					
Chris Spealler, CrossFit Icon and OG				X							X	
Chris Voss, FBI Hostage Negotiator Turned Author & CEO			X									
Coach/CEO Mitch Johns		X		X							X	
Colonel Tim Nye, Marine, Soldier, Officer, Spartan						X	X					

GUEST	Arts/Entertainment/Writing	Business/Career	History/Nation/Law	Life/Family	Media/Technology	Military/Veterans	Outdoors/Adventure	Spirituality/Philosophy	Performance/Effectiveness	Science/Nature	Sports	Health/Wellness/Training
Cory Geishauser, Artist, Author, Friend of Mr. Rogers	X											
Cowboy Gator Magraw, Pro Wrestler with Theatrical Confidence	X											
Dave Berke, Top Gun Fighter Pilot & Combat Veteran						X						
Dave Wagner on Persistent Weight Management												X
Derek Wilson, State Champ									X		X	
Desiree Magee, Mitochondrial Disease Parent/Expert, Co-Founder, Daphne's Lamp				X								X
Diamond Dallas Page, Wrestling Superstar, Actor, Yoga Master	X	X										X
Don Friday, Committed Coach from Coal Country											X	
Dr. Andy Galpin, "Unplugged" Author & "Body of Knowledge" Podcaster					X							X
Dr. Cindra Kamphoff, Peak Performance Expert & Author									X		X	
Dr. Robert Huizenga, "Dr. H" of the NFL & Reality TV	X										X	X

GUEST	Arts/Entertainment/Writing	Business/Career	History/Nation/Law	Life/Family	Media/Technology	Military/Veterans	Outdoors/Adventure	Spirituality/Philosophy	Performance/Effectiveness	Science/Nature	Sports	Health/Wellness/Training
Dr. Tom, The Sponsor Who Trains with the Fighters		X									X	X
Drew Manning, The Fit2Fat2Fit Experimenter												X
Drew Swope, Business Leader Comfortable in His Own Skin		X		X								X
Duane Finley, The Storyteller Who's All In					X						X	
Dustin Pari, *Ghost Hunter* Investigator & Truly Warm Spirit								X				
Earl Granville, Operation Enduring Warrior						X	X					
Eric Stetson of FourBlock						X						
Erica Webster of Dub Fitness						X						X
Erik Lilla, Go-Getting Gymnastics Guru		X		X								
Erin Cafaro, Two-Time Olympic Gold Medal Rower											X	
Frank Luna, Political Staffer Turned Over-Age National Guardsman						X	X					
Frankie Edgar, UFC Champion				X							X	

GUEST	Arts/Entertainment/Writing	Business/Career	History/Nation/Law	Life/Family	Media/Technology	Military/Veterans	Outdoors/Adventure	Spirituality/Philosophy	Performance/Effectiveness	Science/Nature	Sports	Health/Wellness/Training
Fred "Chico" Lager, Former CEO, Ben & Jerry's		x										
Gabriel The Gun, "No Doubt" Musician & Motivational Gangster	x											
Gene Zannetti of Wrestling Mindset		x							x		x	
"Gorgeous George" Garcia of MMAjunkie Radio					x						x	
J.R. Martinez, Soldier, Actor, Speaker, *Dancing with the Stars* Champ						x						
Jack Zerby, Passion & Persistence Personified	x	x		x	x							
Jaclyn DellaTorre, Solid Gold Friend & Brand-New Author of *Chapstick Eater*	x			x								
Jamie Kilstein, Comedian/ Podcaster with Jiu Jitsu Roots	x	x										
Janine Stange, National Anthem Singer in All 50 States	x	x	x									
Jason Stevens, U.S. Marine & Eagle Leader, Team RWB						x						
Jeff Campbell, NFL Veteran											x	

GUEST	Arts/Entertainment/Writing	Business/Career	History/Nation/Law	Life/Family	Media/Technology	Military/Veterans	Outdoors/Adventure	Spirituality/Philosophy	Performance/Effectiveness	Science/Nature	Sports	Health/Wellness/Training
Jody Strittmatter, Wrestling Champ, Coach, Club Co-Founder		x		x							x	
Joe Condora, *Primal Example* Guru of Ancestral Health Techniques												x
Joe De Sena, Founder of Spartan Race		x					x					
Joe Lozito, The Subway Hero Who Stopped a Killer				x								
John Witzing, Endurance Athlete & Founder, The Whiteboard Project							x					x
Johnny Waite, Designer of Live Adventures							x					
Jon Fitch, Veteran UFC & Bellator Fighter											x	
Jonathan Lopez, Operation Enduring Warrior						x	x					
Justin Greskiewicz, Fighter/Trainer/Owner, Stay Fly Muay Thai		x									x	x
Kerry McCoy, So-So Wrestler One Year, NCAA Champ the Next											x	
Kevin Saum on Nearly Dying from Concussion											x	x

GUEST	Arts/Entertainment/Writing	Business/Career	History/Nation/Law	Life/Family	Media/Technology	Military/Veterans	Outdoors/Adventure	Spirituality/Philosophy	Performance/Effectiveness	Science/Nature	Sports	Health/Wellness/Training
Kobi Yamada, NYT Best-Selling Author & CEO of Compendium	x	x										
Kye Smith, Drummer & YouTube Star	x				x							
Kyle Kingsbury, UFC Fighter & Host of Human Optimization Hour					x			x			x	
Kyle Watson, UFC & Ultimate Fighter and Gym Owner		x		x							x	
Larry Hagner, Founder of The Good Dad Project		x		x	x							
Laurie Berkner, Master of Kids' Music	x			x								
Lee Witt, Businessman, Author, Speaker, Band Leader!	x	x										
Legendary Wrestler Cary Kolat											x	
Marc Mero, America's #1 School Presenter	x			x								
Marc Weinstein, Yogi & Look Up! Podcaster					x			x				x
Marisa Zerby, Style Blogger/True Color Expert		x		x								

GUEST	Arts/Entertainment/Writing	Business/Career	History/Nation/Law	Life/Family	Media/Technology	Military/Veterans	Outdoors/Adventure	Spirituality/Philosophy	Performance/Effectiveness	Science/Nature	Sports	Health/Wellness/Training
Matt "The Immortal" Brown, UFC Fighter											x	
Matt Anderson, Film Editor & Spaniard Mainstay Since School Days		x		x	x							
Matt B. Davis of Obstacle Racing Media & The Atlanta Podcast					x		x					
Matt Bradford, USMC Vet, #NoLegsNoVisionNoProblem						x						
Matt Furman, Humble Celebrity Photographer	x			x								
Matt Holmes, Business-Builder at Freedym.com		x										
Matt Marcinek, The Winningest 80-Time Loser Ever									x		x	
Max Major, World-Renowned Mentalist	x											
Michele Jones, Bones Theory Group CEO & Command Sergeant Major (Ret)						x						
Mike Ritland, Navy SEAL Canine Trainer						x						
Mike Salemi, Performance Specialist & Kettlebell Sport World Champ												x

GUEST	Arts/Entertainment/Writing	Business/Career	History/Nation/Law	Life/Family	Media/Technology	Military/Veterans	Outdoors/Adventure	Spirituality/Philosophy	Performance/Effectiveness	Science/Nature	Sports	Health/Wellness/Training
Mike Sarraille, Marine, Navy SEAL, Founder of VETTED						X						
MMA Journalist Ben C.					X						X	
Niyi Sobo, NFL Back, Podcaster, Performance Coach									X		X	
Patrick Murphy, Past "Soldier's Secretary" of the Army						X						
Patty Aubery, Billion-Dollar Brand Builder on a Global Mission		X							X			
Paul Rieckhoff, Founder of IAVA and *Angry Americans* Podcaster					X	X						
Phil Costa, NFL Veteran & Co-Author, *The Transition Playbook*	X	X									X	
Phil Migliarese, Master of Jiu Jitsu & Yoga		X									X	X
Rebecca Wattenschaidt, "Mommy in Heels" Fashion Blogger & Body Positivity Advocate		X		X								
Rich Magee, Plasma Physicist				X						X		
Richard Turner of *Dealt*, World's Best Card Mechanic	X											

GUEST	Arts/Entertainment/Writing	Business/Career	History/Nation/Law	Life/Family	Media/Technology	Military/Veterans	Outdoors/Adventure	Spirituality/Philosophy	Performance/Effectiveness	Science/Nature	Sports	Health/Wellness/Training
Rick Elder, Beyond Clothing		x										
Riley Cote, NHL Enforcer Turned Natural Healing Advocate											x	x
Rod Woodson, NFL Hall of Famer											x	
Rollie Peterkin, Wall Street Trader, MMA Fighter, YouTuber					x		x				x	
Ryan Hawk of *The Learning Leader Show*		x									x	
Ryan Michler, Founder, Order of Man				x	x							
Scott Adams, Creator of Dilbert	x											
Scott Brenneman, Colonel, U.S. Army Reserve, Spanny's Brother, and Ironman				x		x						x
Scott Hebert, *Stoic Mettle* Podcaster					x			x				
Scott Moore, Head Coach, Lock Haven Wrestling				x							x	
Sebastian Terry, "100 Things" Adventurer & Inspirationalist							x					

GUEST	Arts/Entertainment/Writing	Business/Career	History/Nation/Law	Life/Family	Media/Technology	Military/Veterans	Outdoors/Adventure	Spirituality/Philosophy	Performance/Effectiveness	Science/Nature	Sports	Health/Wellness/Training
Sefra Alexandra, The Seed Huntress							x			x		
Shawn Stevenson, Wellness Guru of *The Model Health Show*					x							x
Spencer Lee, State Champion 3.99 Times											x	
Stitch Duran, Legendary Cutman		x		x							x	
Summer Fenton, World-Class Snowboarder							x				x	
TJ Grant, UFC Title Contender				x							x	
Todd Orr, Survivor of a Grizzly Attack (Twice!)							x					
Tom Kwon, Scoutsee		x										
Willie Banks, Track & Field Olympian & Hall of Famer											x	

Books Featured on *The Spaniard Show*
As of this book's publication

BOOK	Arts/Entertainment/Writing	Business/Career	History/Nation/Law	Life/Family	Media/Technology	Military/Veterans	Outdoors/Adventure	Spirituality/Philosophy	Performance/Effectiveness	Science/Nature	Sports	Health/Wellness/Training
11 Rings								x	x		x	
12 Rules for Life								x				
21 Irrefutable Laws of Leadership		x							x			
A Curious Mind	x								x			
A Survival Guide for Life							x		x			
A Walk in the Woods				x			x					
Above the Line									x		x	
Alone on the Wall							x		x			
American Buffalo			x				x			x		
American Wife				x		x						
Astrophysics for People in a Hurry										x		
Awakening Spirits			x					x				
Ben and Jerry's: The Inside Scoop		x										
Born a Crime	x		x	x								
Born Standing Up	x											
Bury My Heart at Wounded Knee			x									

BOOK	Arts/Entertainment/Writing	Business/Career	History/Nation/Law	Life/Family	Media/Technology	Military/Veterans	Outdoors/Adventure	Spirituality/Philosophy	Performance/Effectiveness	Science/Nature	Sports	Health/Wellness/Training
Call Me Ted		x			x						x	
Can't Hurt Me						x			x			x
Chop Wood Carry Water									x			
Eat That Frog									x			
Educated				x								
Extreme Ownership		x				x			x			
Hershey		x	x	x								
How Adam Smith Can Change Your Life								x	x			
How to Change Your Mind	x				x				x			
How to to Fail at Almost Everything and Still Win Big	x				x				x			
How to Win Friends and Influence People		x		x					x			
I Can't Make This Up	x	x		x								
Legacy									x		x	
Make Your Bed						x			x			
Man's Search for Meaning			x	x				x				
Meat Eater							x			x		
Napoleon Hill is On the Air		x							x			
Own the Day, Own Your Life									x			x
Relentless									x		x	

BOOK	Arts/Entertainment/Writing	Business/Career	History/Nation/Law	Life/Family	Media/Technology	Military/Veterans	Outdoors/Adventure	Spirituality/Philosophy	Performance/Effectiveness	Science/Nature	Sports	Health/Wellness/Training
Resilience				x		x						
Rhinoceros Success									x			
Shoe Dog		x									x	
Stephen King - On Writing	x	x										
Success Principles									x			
Team Dog						x			x	x		
The 5 Love Languages				x								
The Art of Learning									x			
The Boys in the Boat			x						x		x	
The Dichotomy of Leadership		x				x			x			
The Energy Bus									x			
The Four Agreements								x				
The Good Neighbor	x			x	x							
The Good Son				x							x	
The Happiness Hypothesis									x	x		
The Obstacle is the Way								x				
The Promise of a Pencil		x										
The Score Takes Care of Itself									x		x	
The Servant		x							x			

BOOK	Arts/Entertainment/Writing	Business/Career	History/Nation/Law	Life/Family	Media/Technology	Military/Veterans	Outdoors/Adventure	Spirituality/Philosophy	Performance/Effectiveness	Science/Nature	Sports	Health/Wellness/Training
The Spartan Way							X		X			
The Talent Code									X			
The Untethered Soul								X				X
The War of Art	X											
The Wisdom of the Native Americans			X					X				
The World's Fittest Book							X				X	X
Think and Grow Rich		X							X			
This is Sparta			X				X				X	
Tiger Woods				X					X		X	
Tribe			X	X								
Unplugged					X							X
When Pride Still Mattered				X							X	
Wooden on Leadership									X		X	

Kids' Books Featured on *The Spaniard Show*
As of this book's publication

BOOK	Arts/Entertainment/Writing	Business/Career	History/Nation/Law	Life/Family	Media/Technology	Military/Veterans	Outdoors/Adventure	Spirituality/Philosophy	Performance/Effectiveness	Science/Nature	Sports	Health/Wellness/Training
After the Fall: How Humpty Dumpty Got Back Up Again									x			
Casey at the Bat			x								x	
Cavekid Birthday			x	x								
Coco				x								
Food Fight Fiesta			x									
Hatchet				x			x					
Holes				x								
I Love You Like …				x								
It's Trevor Noah: Born a Crime	x		x	x								
Mikey and the Dragons				x					x			
Mirth Meets Earth			x							x		
The Bad Seed									x			
The Breadwinner			x	x								

BOOK	Arts/Entertainment/Writing	Business/Career	History/Nation/Law	Life/Family	Media/Technology	Military/Veterans	Outdoors/Adventure	Spirituality/Philosophy	Performance/Effectiveness	Science/Nature	Sports	Health/Wellness/Training
The Good Egg									x			
The Outsiders				x								
The Story of Ferdinand								x				
Way of the Warrior Kid: From Wimpy to Warrior the Navy SEAL Way				x					x			
Way of the Warrior Kid: Marc's Mission				x					x			
What Do You Do with a Chance?									x			
What Do You Do with a Problem?									x			
Where the Red Fern Grows				x			x					
Wonder				x								
You Are Special				x								

Acknowledgments

I'd like to thank:

My parents and family for laying the foundation of who I am.

My wife, Amanda, for co-piloting this ride. It's no easy task.

My kids, Gracie and Rocky. You've expanded my heart. Your energy and wonder inspire me every day, and I can only hope to replicate it. You give me greater purpose and have reignited my love of learning and teaching.

My friend, creative partner, shaman, therapist, advisor - and everything else that goes along with building a business, Dread.

I'm grateful for all the books, authors, hosts and learning resources I've utilized over the course of my life. This book is about learning, and without them it wouldn't be possible.

Our slice of the Brenneman fam

About the Author

Charlie "The Spaniard" Brenneman is a former
Division I wrestler, Spanish teacher and UFC fighter who
lives in his native Pennsylvania with his wife Amanda and
their children Gracie and Rocky. His mission to embody and
inspire lifelong learning has led him to podcasting, writing
and speaking.

I'd love to hear what you
think of the book!
Just leave a review
on Amazon or reach out
on social media
          @charliespaniard
      Thanks!
      - Spaniard

Made in the USA
Middletown, DE
08 January 2020